TRUST YOUR VOICE

A
ROADMAP
TO
FOCUS
AND
INFLUENCE

SYLVIE LÉGÈRE

AND

KERI WYATT KENT

Trust Your Voice

A Roadmap To Focus And Influence

By Sylvie Légère
and Keri Wyatt Kent
Copyright © 2021 by Sylvie Légère
Cover design by Tommy Owen.
Interior design by Carol Davis.
Published by The Policy Circle in cooperation with A Powerful Story.
The Policy Circle
1189 Wilmette Avenue #210
Wilmette, IL 60091
www.thepolicycircle.org

The Policy Circle name and logo are trademarks of The Policy Circle.
The publisher is not responsible for websites (or their content) that are not owned
by the publisher. All web citations were accurate at time of publication.
ISBN 978-1-737-4473-0-6

To my children Daphné, Pascale, and Félix
and my husband, Todd,
and to the many people who have crossed my path
and made a positive impact in my life.

Table of Contents

*We keep moving forward—opening up new doors and doing new things—
because we are curious.
And curiosity keeps leading us down new paths.* —Walt Disney

PART I

Strengthening Your Foundation

Confidence. Trust. Where do these qualities come from? Trust is essential if we are to become all that we are meant to be.

How can you trust that your voice matters? How can you begin to have the confidence to trust in yourself, others, and even the process of building something significant? That's what this book is about.

This book will guide you toward both personal and professional growth. Use it to frame your discussions with a mentor or with someone you are mentoring. Use it to "mentor yourself," that is, to reflect on your life, your goals, your growth. Use it with a group of people you'd like to grow deeper with. Or use it to go deeper in conversation with people you value. Consider this a tool to help you grow and fuel your confidence in yourself, in others, in the future.

In the chapters that follow (in Part One), we will explore seven essential trusts that we must develop in order to have greater confidence in our own voice. Each of these "trusts" fuels your confidence. I view them as seven practices to build a firm foundation and keep moving forward. None of us ever "achieves" perfection or ultimate success. Success is a journey, a continuous process. When we let go and trust, we can embrace our purpose and help others to achieve their goals as well. We can move forward, soaring on our strengths.

At the end of each chapter, you'll find a Trust Challenge—an opportunity to both reflect and act upon what you've just read. The questions might also guide a discussion of the book with others.

In Part Two, we'll discuss some practical tools for expanding your influence and engaging in constructive conversations towards solutions.

Over the past six years, my co-founders Angela Braly and Kathy Hubbard and I built The Policy Circle, a national nonprofit organization that engages women and helps them to find their voice and trust it. We've seen the value that women bring to shaping public policy, because they bring a fresh perspective to the table. This book is about what I have learned by trying new things as an entrepreneur—succeeding sometimes and learning by mistakes at other times. I hope that my story will help you to do the same.

Chapter 1

Trust: How Can We Build It?

While I wrote this book, America faced unprecedented challenges: presidential impeachment hearings; the COVID-19 pandemic and ensuing shutdown of the U.S. economy; a historic surge in unemployment; and racial tension and social unrest resulting in protests, looting, burning of Bibles, defacing of statues, and destruction of property—even an attack on the U.S. Capitol. As a result of this period of chaos, competing narratives, and growing division, you may find yourself asking, "Whom can I trust?"

Increasingly, you've probably wondered about the roles of government, businesses, individuals, and the media, and the calls to reform these institutions that make up the fabric of our daily lives. In the midst of such rapid change, the deluge of information and misinformation feels staggering.

Like many Americans, you may feel it is hard to know which sources are telling the truth. Is whatever television news you watch accurate? Does the media have an agenda? Are newspapers reliable? Trusted sources are difficult to come by, and this increased distrust undermines the authority and credibility of government, institutions, elected officials, and the media.

Trust is essential, but it seems to be slipping out of our culture. Increasingly, we mistrust the government, the media, even other people—especially those who seem to be different from us.

According to the article "Building Trust in America," we have a crisis of trust in our country.

> American National Election Studies began asking about trust in the federal government in 1958, when 75 percent of the population demonstrated trust in government. These levels of trust eroded during the late 1960s and 1970s, reflecting the turbulence of the Vietnam War, Watergate, and economic struggles. During the 1980s and 1990s, trust in the government fluctuated, tending to coincide with good economic growth. It reached a three-decade high shortly after the 9/11 attacks, but since 2007 less than 30 percent of respondents have said they can trust the federal government always or most of the time. In particular, the *2019 Gallup Confidence in Institutions* survey found Americans have the least amount of confidence in Congress, with only 11 percent saying they trust Congress "a great deal," and 52 percent saying they have very little or no confidence in Congress.[1]

When people lack trust in each other and institutions, "they are less likely to comply with laws and regulations, pay taxes, tolerate different viewpoints or ways of life, contribute to economic vitality, resist the appeals of demagogues, or support their neighbors . . . They are less likely to create and invent."[2] Citizens will be unwilling to cooperate freely if they do not believe that others are responsible and trustworthy or that their rights are guaranteed and protected.

So how can this lack of trust be solved? How will we progress, individually and as a society, if trust is gone? It begins with dialogue. "Trust builds when people feel they are part of a community- or society-wide enterprise that takes their concerns and voices into account."[3] And dialogue happens when people trust their own voices enough to share their opinions and work together to find solutions.

---

1   from https://docs.google.com/document/d/1WiyDk0rQ8nqvdsnvVJb5IuFqdOC-i0jbyug_BkEEKVY/edit
2   See "Six Ways to Repair Declining Trust" on the Stanford Social Innovation Review at: https://ssir.org/articles/entry/six_ways_to_repair_declining_social_trust
3   Ibid.

All of us desire significance and purpose. To reach these goals, we must have trust in ourselves and others to think and make decisions that will lead to positive outcomes in the long term. But how do we develop trust?

In his classic book *Man's Search for Meaning*, Holocaust survivor Victor Frankl wrote, "Everything can be taken from a man but one thing: the last of human freedoms—to choose one's attitude in any given set of circumstances."[4]

For many years, I kept waiting for confidence to somehow show up. Eventually, I realized that I needed to trust my own voice, even when it was shaking. I needed to let go of doing it all alone and intentionally surround myself with people who I could trust to help me achieve my potential. I also needed to be willing to help them ignite their potential.

Giving Women Something Better

In 2013, my husband and I attended several conferences featuring discussions and research on the impact of public policies on entrepreneurial values in our society. One event featured Campbell Brown, Susan Crow, and Christina Hoff-Summers. At this "women's event," they talked about women in politics, policy, and economics and the entrepreneurial culture in the U.S. The topic fascinated me, and I wanted to share it, so I invited some friends to attend it with me.

We came back energized to learn more and participate more. My friend Beth Feeley suggested we take it a step further than just attending an event. It would be even better if we could organize something with women in our neighborhood. Beth suggested we get together and determine who we are and figure out who would like to talk about ideas in policy, economic theories, and current public policies impacting people's desire to start and grow businesses, to engage in their community. What if we didn't even have to go downtown to have a discussion on important public policy issues?

So, a few friends and I decided we'd organize an evening, which we called Political Fiber. Juicing was popular at the time, so I said, "Come over to my house to drink green juice and vodka and discuss the future direction of America." Why not, right? Beth and another friend, Joan, who are much more extroverted than I am, invited people. And 15 women came!

4 Frankel, Viktor. *Man's Search for Meaning*. Boston: Beacon Press. 1959. 66.

We all sat in my living room, looking at each other and silently asking, Okay, now what? To start, we went around the room and each woman shared why she was there. That's where I discovered the power of the round-table discussion model of going around the room systematically. Giving space for all women, even the quiet ones, to share perspectives, ideas, hesitations, experiences on complex problems that our society faces, is empowering. Women are eager to learn and engage in substantive discussion about the way the world works.

At that first meeting, as we went around the room, a theme quickly emerged. Most of the women felt there was no space to speak up, to strengthen their voices. Over and over, people said things like, "I come from a political family, but I quickly learned that you can get attacked for just asking questions. I've just learned to be quiet." Or "I learned not to make waves, to be polite." Or "I came to understand that asking questions or talking about things I thought should change could be triggers for some."

Although I'm an introvert, I have a strong "reformer"[5] personality, and I wanted to give us women something better. We decided we would get together again. To prepare for that gathering, we asked people to brainstorm a name for the group, something besides Political Fiber. We also agreed to read a book and discuss it. Because we were interested in economics and policy, we thought *Free to Choose* by Milton and Rose Friedman might make for some interesting discussion.

As I prepared for the next meeting, I was talking to a neighbor, and he told me that Rose Friedman, Milton Friedman's wife, was a prominent economist of her own, and she really challenged Milton Friedman. She was all about having these economic conversations. So, I thought maybe we should call ourselves the Rose Friedman Society. (A name that ultimately didn't stick!)

---

5 The Reformer is Type One in the Enneagram Test which I encourage you to take to help you define/describe your own personality. Ones are people of practical action—they wish to be *useful* in the best sense of the word. On some level of consciousness, they feel that they "have a mission" to fulfill in life, if only to try their best to reduce the disorder they see in their environment. https://www.enneagraminstitute.com/type-1/

I was pleasantly surprised that 25 people came to the next meeting! As word spread, we asked people to read the first four chapters of *Free to Choose*. A group of 25 was too big for discussion, so we divided into four groups, then regrouped at the end to summarize what each of us had talked about. Breaking into smaller groups gave everyone in the room a chance to talk and share their perspectives. Knowing they'd have to present a summary of their smaller group discussion kept everyone on their toes.

The energy in the room was just unbelievable.

It was an event where women could use their minds, stretch their intellect. They felt valued, energized, respected, and connected. They each felt that they had a mind of their own.

That's when I realized, I'm on to something.

For our next meeting, the women in the group said they wanted to talk about healthcare—a big topic, especially because this was 2014. The Affordable Care Act, also known as Obamacare, had been signed into law using a presidential executive order in March of 2010, but most of it had gone into effect January 1, 2014. Healthcare premiums were rising dramatically for some people, making it a hot-button issue for everyone.

The experience of reading the first four chapters of a book with the group showed me that we needed to have something to ground the conversation. Saying we'd discuss something so broad as "healthcare" meant we were flooded with information. It was hard to know what sources were reliable since opinions abound. I started sending all kinds of articles to the group. I wasn't a healthcare expert, so as I did research, I simply forwarded the information I found to the group. We had mountains of material to read. One woman invited an expert in health insurance, and we had some politicians lined up to discuss the legislation, but we were overloaded with information.

I quickly realized we needed a brief.

A policy brief is not a white paper but a shorter document that sums up the facts on an issue—how did we get here and what are we trying to solve—and outlines possible policy changes (i.e. legislation) that might be used to address that issue. Policy briefs often make a recommendation to lawmakers, but I wanted a brief that showed all sides of the issue and the ramifications of what different options might be, how much our federal government is already doing and spending, how to research the involvement of state government and feature local solutions and engagement of privately owned businesses and nonprofits. Creating a readable, concise document that examined the various sides of the issue would keep our discussions more focused and allow us to fact-check the information we included in our discussion. Beth, who helped organize those early meetings, was instrumental in helping write and shape the briefs we began to produce.

I also quickly realized that we needed a better way to communicate. We had a Facebook group, we had emails, and we tried to use online invitations to let people invite friends, but it became unmanageable. We had to be a little more organized and communicate privately with people who were enthused about meeting to talk about public policy!

Gathering with Women Who Gather Women

At about that time, I attended an event organized by the American Enterprise Institute. There, I met Angela Braly, former chief executive officer for WellPoint, Inc., a large health insurance company now known as Anthem. We met during cocktail hour, and, since she was in the healthcare industry, I told her about my experience with Foov Fitness, a company I had started to engage people with intellectual disabilities to exercise. And I also mentioned my women's group that was meeting to discuss policy, including healthcare.

When I described the idea behind this group—reading and researching relevant material and then gathering as a group to discuss it—Angela told me, "That sounds like a Bible study." And I said, "What is that?" Because although I'd grown up Catholic, I'd never heard of people getting together to read Scripture this way, to get guidance and introspection, and to talk about it. So, she sent me a little Bible study booklet, and I was fascinated. I'd never seen one before. Reading through it and understanding how it worked gave me the confidence to say, I want to ask people to read material, ponder good questions, then gather to discuss it.

Angela told me that she had also gathered women around policy addressing poverty in Indiana. She introduced me to Kathy Hubbard, also from

Indiana, with whom she had organized the event. They agreed that women seemed to be peripheral to the public policy dialogue and that most conferences confined our participation to so-called women's issues: pay equity, work leave, education, and representation. We wanted a place where women could learn, discover their voices, and be heard on economic issues..

The three of us had a common trait: whenever we see a situation, we take the lead to do something to change what needs to be changed. We convened to define a vision for groups of women across the country to gather in their communities and take leadership roles in the public policy dialogue by openly sharing their views on the impact of public policy on creativity in an open economy.

Angela and Kathy believed in the model that I stumbled upon of women coming together in small groups to host discussions based on facts. We searched for other organizations that were doing something similar. After all, the three of us had each started groups for women to discuss policy. And we'd happened to meet? Surely there were others doing the same thing. But although we found many groups that focused on political parties and candidates training and inviting speakers, we couldn't find any that focused on grassroots policy education and discussion designed to develop the leadership skills of everyday women.

So, in 2015, we launched The Policy Circle (thepolicycircle.org), a nonprofit, nonpartisan grassroots educational organization. We created a website for members to access a library of policy briefs, which we co-wrote with experts. Rather than doing research themselves, group members simply have to read the brief and come prepared to share their perspectives and listen to the views of others on the policy and how they relate to their family, their work, and their community. That seems simple, but it flips the model. Women are asked to form a circle, meet five times, self-facilitate, and learn about and discuss topics they are not familiar with. It requires courage and leadership. And the experience builds social capital.

A circle starts with three people, and each invites one person, which makes six. Then all six of them invite one more person, so you've got twelve people. That's a circle. The Policy Circle was launched to engage women, but men are not excluded if a group chooses to include them.

When you are invited to a Policy Circle, you know that you're going to speak. The experience is transformational. You read a policy brief differently when you know that you will have to present your understanding of the issues. You internalize the issue and compose your own way of expressing your views. You gain trust in yourself. You gain confidence.

To get started, you're given a simple question to frame your ideas: What is the lens you read this brief through? How does that lens impact the way you see it? What actions would you take to engage with this issue in your community and in your company? The round table discussion model to share the lenses through which women understand an issue also gives women an opportunity to share their life focus. You find out meaningful things about each other. You discover the multiple hats and experiences that women bring to the table: perhaps they grew up in housing projects, or lived abroad, or studied biomedical engineering, or started their own business. Maybe they are healthcare professionals, or financial planners. They might be caring for elderly parents with Alzheimer's or children with special needs, and juggling that with a career. The model and the invitation to talk about the lens through which you are reading the brief gives you the chance to speak up, to use your voice, and to trust it.

I have found that women are very focused on the day-to-day and the busyness of their lives. American women especially gravitate to the to-do list. They want to do something right away, they want to act. That's great, but we want to invite women into higher levels of leadership, into navigating complex issues and leading with ideas and vision before getting things done. The Policy Circle invites them to first reflect, connect the dots, and then plan what would be the most impactful, rather than focusing on temporary fixes. They learn to take a step back to look at the root causes of problems rather than rushing to quick "band-aid" solutions.

This simple process of reflection and planning helps people to build trust in themselves enough to act. For many, it is the beginning of learning to trust their voice, even when it shakes.

Trust Challenge:

What issue matters deeply to you? What's one thing you can do to learn more about that issue? This week, reach out to someone who might share your interest in that issue and just have a conversation about it. Ask them about the lens they view the issue through.

Gathering to discuss ideas in a group, whether it is for a book club, Bible study or Policy Circle, is a powerful way to learn. What is your experience with this type of group? What specific benefits do you think such gatherings provide?

Chapter 2

Trust the Features of Human Nature

I did not grow up in a family of entrepreneurs, but rather, a political family. My mother worked full time for the Canadian government in international development and also managed information services to elected officials (or parliamentarians) at Canada's Library of Parliament (like the U.S. Library of Congress), before moving on to leading library/information services at a university.

My mother was a modern woman in the 1970s—she took on roles in information technology (when IT was just in its infancy), she went to international conferences, she changed careers. She modeled for me how to always be learning, and how to step out of your comfort zone, stay humble, and care for the people you love without limits.

My father was a lawyer and politician, a larger-than-life character, beloved in our town and region of Canada. I grew up in Hull, now called Gatineau, Quebec. French-speaking Hull was the neighboring city of Ottawa, the capital of Canada located just across the river in the province of Ontario. Today, the Canadian national capital region is the birthplace of Instant Pot and Shopify, but it is primarily a government town. My father was the mayor of Hull from the time I was 12 until I was 22.

Even now, 30 years after he has left office, people remember my father and still refer to him as the mayor. He's a charming person, lively and engaging. If people meet him once, they remember him, and their comment is always, "He made me feel good about myself." A lot of his energy has always been directed toward the public because that was his career. That is who he is. However, the confidence he gave to others, I didn't necessarily feel.

Growing up in a small town, I was always known as the mayor's daughter. I grew up with him in public office, and our family lived in his shadow. I never really felt like I was my own person. No matter who you are, you're always "the daughter of…" and never just you. That's life—the blessing and the curse of living in a human community. People assign labels. Being a shy person, I rejected the "mayor's daughter" label instead of embracing it. I lived in Canada but attended a lycée Français (a French school managed by the French government). I felt disconnected from the city that my dad was running. However, one thing he taught me that marked me and that I have always valued was this—the voices of all people matter.

My dad is curious about people and genuinely loves to learn as much as possible about them and their perspectives. He brings out the best in everyone that he encounters. I joke that my dad could run for village president in my town here in Illinois and he would win. As a politician, he had an open-door policy. Each Wednesday, his office was open for anyone to come see him, and his phone number was in the phone book, which meant that people would call us at home, after business hours, about snow removal, domestic cases, all kinds of stuff. So he was known and liked by all the citizens in our town of 61,000 people.

He was also a man of vision. As mayor, my dad pushed for a museum to be built on our side of the river. He also pushed for that museum to be turned toward our city instead of having its back to the city (by facing the river and Ottawa on the opposite bank).

He represented the town with pride, asking that it be fully recognized as part of the greater national capital region and as a representation of the specificity of the French-speaking province of Quebec. In those days, there was quite a bit of animosity between and English Canada and French-speaking Quebec as a strong separatist movement thrived in Quebec, and my dad was part of that movement. (A referendum to make Quebec a separate country at that time was voted down by a very narrow margin.) Consequently, he was not invited, nor fully welcome in Ottawa—but he never backed down. He took pride in and saw the importance of small gestures like shaking the Ottawa mayor's hand on the bridge on Canada Day or welcoming Pope Jean Paul II in Hull during his visit to Canada to amplify the visibility of French-speaking Quebec.

Being the kid of a politician or someone with a public life means that you are also in public life. You wake up to go to school only to find journalists and union workers protesting at your door, or you are looking for a summer job and you discover that you can't work as a lifeguard for the city pool when you just spent your whole year getting the Red Cross certification. (My working for the city in any capacity would have been considered nepotism and therefore was not allowed.)

I remember attending my father's "work events," such as Christmas parties at retirement homes, visits to fire stations, police-force celebrations, ribbon cuttings at housing co-ops. At the time, I was an introverted teenager. I only wanted privacy, anonymity. I wanted my last name to not be recognized. But today, I am grateful for the gift of being part of building a community. Because of what my dad taught and modeled, "everyone's perspective matters" is a core value embodied in The Policy Circle.

Seizing Opportunities
After I graduated from the lycée in economics, I wasn't sure what I was going to study at university. I struggled to decide what to major in. I was literally standing in line to register for school, looking at the descriptions of different majors. Based on the short description of a specialized program that offered a work-study co-op, I decided, right there in line in the registrar's office, to pursue a degree in management information systems. I would be in school one semester, and then work for one semester to gain practical experience and earn money to pay for my studies.

That choice forced me to learn English, pushed me to discover the kind of work environment that suited me, and opened the door to jobs at a time when unemployment was at 12 percent in Quebec, and 9.7 percent in Canada.[6] I had the opportunity to work as an intern in different types of

---

6 See https://www.statcan.gc.ca/eng/dai/btd/othervisuals/other017. and 9.7% in Canada https://www150.statcan.gc.ca/n1/daily-quotidien/170707/cg-a003-eng.htm

companies, including Bell Canada, SHL SystemHouse (a consulting firm), and IBM—all while earning my degree.

Early on, I realized that I was a project person. I wanted a job that would change often, and I wanted to travel the world. My first job out of college was with the global consulting firm, Accenture. I joined the Ottawa office, and because I was bilingual, I was assigned to Canada Post Projects as part of Government Services. In other words, I worked for the Canadian post office. I absolutely hated it, and I could not believe that I was stuck working on systems that sorted mail. It seemed so mundane, so boring, so bureaucratic. However, I was a valuable associate because I was bilingual, competent, hardworking, and committed to quality outputs.

At a work social event, I learned about the firm sponsoring employees in a postgraduate program at Northwestern University's Learning Science Institute in Chicago. I am still incredibly grateful to my mentor Graham Gordon and the partners in the Ottawa office for sponsoring me to earn a master's in Computer Science with a specialization in the Learning Sciences. Seizing that opportunity, with the support of others, changed the course of my life.

When I came to the United States to go to graduate school, something changed. I remember driving here by myself in my little 1987 Toyota Corolla. I felt free; I felt empowered. When I came to the states, I observed a very different culture than the one I'd grown up in. French people are, in a word, skeptical. We don't believe things right away. We never take things at face value. We can be extremely cynical. On the other hand, we value engaging in conversation about how the world works or doesn't work. French people are less hesitant to ask deeper questions about perspectives, and to disagree vehemently but to still be friends. (These are of course generalizations.)[7]

What struck me about Americans was their unwavering optimism. No matter what situation or industry, most Americans seemed to have little to no skepticism of anyone they'd decided (correctly or not) was "on their side." Perhaps the fact that I went to school at Northwestern University, located in a suburb of Chicago, colored my view of Americans. Chicago, though

---

7 For more on cultural differences, I recommend Erin Meyer's book *The Culture Map.* See https://erinmeyer.com/books/the-culture-map/

a big city, is one that values hard work and has a friendly, Midwestern feel, and people here seem less jaded than those on the East or West Coast. But overall, Americans are much more optimistic than the French, or even Canadians.

Coming to the U.S. the year that Netscape, the first internet browser, was launched, I was struck by the audacity of people around me, the desire to innovate and to start businesses that would improve the way we live. I did not have the vocabulary to describe this uniquely American trait called entrepreneurship or the free-enterprise system that fuels creativity. I did not realize that I had developed a new skill: seizing opportunities.

As a French-Canadian Québecoise, I was an outsider for about 10 years. My good friends were also expats. While living in Chicago and going to graduate school, I was introduced to Todd Ricketts. Long story short, we eventually got married. My perceptions of Americans as optimistic and entrepreneurial were confirmed by meeting Todd's family. They are all very hard working and have strong personalities. They are people who take action, whether by getting behind a good cause, investing in a promising business, or starting a new business.

My father-in-law, Joe Ricketts, is incredibly innovative. From a small financial services company in Nebraska, he innovated and grew. He created a company, Ameritrade (now part of Schwab) that was the first to provide individuals an inexpensive way to trade stocks themselves and manage their finances in a new way. His work literally changed the way ordinary people invest and save, and opened up opportunities for countless people. He wrote a book called *The Harder You Work, The Luckier You Get*. The title sums up his approach to life.

My brother-in-law Peter became governor of Nebraska. My sister-in-law Laura has worked hard for marriage equality for the LGBTQ community. My other brother-in-law Tom had a successful financial services company. They are always focused on growth and innovation.

In 2009, this family became the owners of the largest franchise in major-league baseball, the Chicago Cubs, and I found myself calling Wrigley Field my second home. Growing up in Canada, I had not been exposed to the enthusiasm that Americans have for sports. In the years since then, I have come to appreciate the value of sports to build relationships across everything—ages, demographics, socioeconomic backgrounds. Sports bring all different sorts of people together. I didn't have that appreciation until I became part of the Cubs family.

Watching Todd's family seize opportunities and take risks made it easier for me to try new things—like launching The Policy Circle. Innovation and hard work are part of the family culture, and that inspired me.

As wonderful as the family's influence is on me, I continue to bring an outsider's perspective to American culture. Americans take a lot for granted and judge themselves harshly. What some may perceive as shallowness, I see as friendliness and welcoming; what may be perceived as arrogance is a strong desire to solve problems to get stuff done. Americans innovate and create. They take risks, invest in ideas and remain optimistic.

I have come to learn and value the founding principles of America that are actually what explains the boundless optimism and take-charge culture of Americans. I will quote here my new friend Jack Miller, who started the Jack Miller Center for the Teaching of America's Founding Principles and History:

> America is a country that was itself born with a mission and a vision of the freedom of each individual embedded as the reason for its being, the document declaring its independence from its mother country. In the second paragraph of our Declaration of Independence are the thirty-six words that would forever change how a free people would think of themselves: "We hold these Truths to be self-evident, that all Men are created equal, that they are endowed by their Creator with certain unalienable Rights, that among these are Life, Liberty, and the Pursuit of Happiness."
>
> It says all men, meaning all individuals. Then in the first paragraph of our Constitution, it states, "WE THE PEOPLE of the United States, in order to form a more perfect Union, establish Justice, insure domestic Tranquility, provide for the common defense, promote the general Welfare, and secure the Blessings of Liberty to

ourselves and our posterity, do ordain and establish this Constitution for the United States of America."

They established the first (national) *written* constitution in the world,[8] and the first government formed by the consent of the governed. America was built on a certain culture of self-reliance, hard work, the rule of law, and the belief that "all Men are created equal" and have an opportunity to improve their position in life through their own effort. That vision for America is a constant work in progress that will never be finished in our lifetime. But as it says in The Ethics of the Fathers (Pirkei Avot), "It is not for you to complete the task, but neither are you free to stand aside from it." [9]

10 Features of Human Nature

In learning to trust our own voice, we must realize that within us, and within every human being, there is a capacity for good and a capacity for evil. Each of us can behave in ways that are altruistic and kind and also selfish and even mean. This should not surprise us—because if you look into your own heart and soul, you'll see both of these sides in yourself. In fact, I would say that there are 10 features of human nature, which we simply cannot ignore. The first five are positive; the last five are difficult truths and may seem negative. They are:

- Empathy - Humans have empathy and compassion.
- Love - Humans want to feel loved, valued by others.
- Competition - Humans love competition and recognition.
- Connection - Humans want to feel connected with others and are designed to thrive in community.
- Creativity - Humans are creative. The human mind's capacity for optimization and problem solving is amazing.
- Harm - Humans all have a capacity to harm, especially when we are not held accountable for our actions or when we're overcome by fear.

---

8   See https://constitutioncenter.org/learn/educational-resources/historical-documents/perspectives-on-the-constitution-constitutions-around-the-world
9   Miller, Jack. *Born to Be Free*. Rowman and Littlefield, 2018, 5.

- Easiest Path - Humans tend to follow the path of least resistance.
- Control - Humans want control of their circumstances, environment, and the people around them.
- Groupthink - Conformity and groupthink tend to prevail. Humans believe rumors and will often "go with the crowd" out of fear.[10]
- Fear - Humans fear the unknown and can often become trapped in this loop of ignorance, which sometimes leads them to inflict suffering on others.

These are simply observations, and there are likely other ways to describe general human nature. But I often find that people are surprised by the fact that other people can be mean or selfish. They are even more surprised when they discover it in themselves. We've all had that experience of saying something thoughtless, or even mean, and wishing we could hit "rewind" and take back what we said or did. Almost everyone, at some time, has said something they regret.

Knowing that everyone has the capacity to be either kind or cruel can actually help us. We can right-size our expectations and also keep ourselves in check. These laws of human nature can also predict how we will handle tools, technology, relationships, or the unintended consequences of government directives. In discussions on public policy, these simple human tendencies need to be taken into account. For instance, the federal CARES Act relief package for COVID-19 in 2020, which offered unemployed workers an extra $600 a week, may have had the unintended consequence of encouraging people to not return to work.[11]

As James Madison wrote in *The Federalist Papers*, "If men were angels, no government would be necessary. If angels were to govern men, neither external nor internal controls on government would be necessary."[12]

When deciding to enter public office or assume a higher level of leadership, it is helpful to preview in our mind how these laws of human nature

---

10 For a humorous look at groupthink, watch this old Candid Camera clip at https://vimeo.com/277929528.

11 This article provides an interesting perspective on this issue: https://www.npr.org/2020/05/26/861906616/when-returning-to-your-job-means-a-cut-in-pay)

12 See http://bit.ly/MenandAngels

are likely to play out in our bubble. The following clichés help us preview and process adversity that we will most likely face when we step up:

- No good deed goes unpunished.
- Guilt by association
- They start shooting when you're over the target.

That's not to say all of human nature is bad. We have a capacity for both good and evil, and when we make an effort to cultivate the good, we grow. We move forward in our lives, our relationships, our careers. We also begin to not only trust our voice, but also to have compassion for ourselves and others.

Notice Both Strengths and Weaknesses

The positive traits of human beings could almost be a self-compassion mantra. Most of us want to be positive, encouraging people, but we need to remind ourselves to do so. We have to live with intention. If we embrace the positive side of human nature, we can tell ourselves:

- I am loved, I am valued, I feel connected.
- I am creative enough to do what's right and good, even if it's hard.
- I treat others like I want to be treated (compassion).
- I have an urgency to impact.

Just as we need to embrace our own strengths we are able to embrace and propel the strengths of others.

The negative traits are just as true, but our awareness of them should lead us to resist them when we notice them in ourselves. Instead of pretending we're perfect or that we never make mistakes, we can admit that we have tendencies to let our fear do the talking or just blurt out critiques without thinking. To counter this, we can tell ourselves:

- I am not afraid; I seek to understand.
- I am curious, not furious.
- I can surrender control.
- I have a mind of my own.
- I am authentic and truthful.

While the only person you can control is yourself, understanding human nature will help you in relationships with others as well. When you set up a process, an internal or a public policy, keep the laws of human nature in mind. You can take a moment to ask:

- What is the path of least resistance that people will take?
- Are we treating people like sheep, or will people be in control, creative, unique?
- Will people feel ignorant or empowered?
- Does it foster competition and innovation or kill it slowly?
- Will people feel loved, valued, connected?
- Do we treat people the way we want to be treated?

My list is missing one aspect of human nature: What explains the despicable behavior of some people on social media and this capacity for bullying and humiliating others, spreading lies? Maybe it comes into play in people who have so little control over their lives that they need to control others. Social media has given a megaphone to those who seek control. It is easier to destroy than to build; it is easier to point the flaws in others than to focus on our own actions. The only thing that we can do is resist, counter and not give it oxygen by engaging. But awareness of human capacity for fear and self-centered thinking can help us to resist it.

People have a capacity for service and a capacity for selfishness, whether in business or in government. I try to remind myself that those in government and in business are all humans.

When I first came to the States, I noticed that Americans seem to want to believe the best about people and situations, even when there is plenty of evidence to the contrary. The idealism I observed in American culture surprised me. I have to admit, I'm kind of a cynic. I see people who say that they are in favor of public schools yet send their kids to the most elitist schools. I see people who claim to be environmentalists but love their Keurig coffee makers, take out food containers and drink bottled water at an Earth conference. I see people who say they favor an increase in minimum wage, but refuse to think about the impact on small, local businesses staffed with part-timers. I see the media twisting words, not to educate people about laws and process, but just to ignite outrage and a sense of chaos—a sense of lack of control.

Part of learning to trust your voice is figuring out what it is you really think, to not fall for headlines or sound bites that are meant to outrage rather than inform. To do that, you have to understand human nature and your own personality. Are you a cynic like me, or do you tend to believe others? Do your stated beliefs on issues match your actions?

Human beings have a basic desire for security, love, and control. In order to get those needs met, we might do things that hurt others, out of self-preservation or self-protection. If one of these gets out of balance, then we get out of balance. We might do things that we would not expect from ourselves!

Bringing Out the Best in People

To learn to trust human nature, we need to acknowledge both the good and bad. We need to embrace reality. Evil results from fear and perpetuates fear. But when we choose to be generous and helpful, when we choose the good, we bring that out in other people. We can build trust and still be realistic.

Through my work with The Policy Circle, I met an amazing entrepreneur, Heidi Ganahl. She's involved politically, and she's a regent of the Colorado University network. When I met her, she had just finished writing a book, *She Factor,* and was creating a business plan to launch it. She told me she would be in Chicago to promote it. I said, without hesitation, "Let me host a book launch."

I'm always about bringing people together. It makes me happy to make connections. That's what The Policy Circle is all about. It's not just to raise awareness or give people information. Rather, it's about what happens when people gather and share their perspectives and feed off of one another's energy. I thought this would be a great opportunity to introduce her concept of the "She Factor."

We hosted the launch party right before a baseball game in our suite at Wrigley Field. I made it a mother-daughter event and reached out to various networks in business, school, and nonprofits. About 50 people attended, mothers with their daughters or nieces, and in one case, her son. People seemed happy to be there, chatting over hot dogs. After Heidi's talk, there was a little time before the game, so I decided to do what we do in our Policy Circle meetings.

I said, "Why don't we go around the room, and everyone can introduce themselves and tell us what they do? Tell us about your organization." In my experience, giving a space for women to introduce themselves not only professionally but also to introduce their passion project or engagement allows for connection and relationship building. The same thing happens each time a Policy Circle gathers. It supercharges people's ability to connect. And that, too, is a truth about human nature. Humans crave meaningful connections.

The idea behind The Policy Circle is not just educating but equipping. Informed and constructive conversations about public policy open the door for building meaningful relationships and compassion. Through conversations on ideas we learn to trust our capacity for thought leadership, for establishing connections and for starting to engage with policy makers at various levels. We may lean in to participate in an advisory task force, build a relationship with our government representatives, publish opinion pieces or even run for office.

History Teaches Us

When I had my children, I was surprised at how giving birth triggered a very strong instinct to protect that child. When you become a parent, watching the news on television or reading the newspaper becomes personal. I became more highly aware of bad things that happened in the world around me and more fearful they would happen to me or my family. It felt like there were so many ways my children could get injured, and I was helpless to prevent them all, no matter how vigilant I was. No matter how much I tried, I could not prevent them from scraping their knees or feeling sad on occasion.

Being a parent sharpens your sense of empathy. It also introduces you to worrying about things you never gave a second thought to before. I became attuned to human suffering around the world, which I had no power to stop. I asked why. What made humans inflict such suffering on other humans? How was the genocide in Bosnia, Rwanda, or the Holocaust, even possible? How could humans be able to humiliate, torture, kill another? As a parent, these questions took on deeper significance. Why was one of the laws of human nature that we will cause harm to others?

That question haunts me.

My StrengthsFinder test[13] indicates that I am a strong Context person. I seek to understand what has been done in the past to inform current situations. I think I have passed along my love of history to my children. My daughter, who is now 17, has enjoyed biographies since she learned to read in second grade. Then she started to focus on World War II novels. She is fascinated with the stories of people, countries, and governments of that era.

When reading about human history, you realize that human suffering plays a part of human history. There has never been a time in which humans did not inflict pain on others. Unfortunately, throughout history, humans have attempted to control other humans in horrible ways. In 1971, social psychologist Philip Zimbardo ran what was called the Stanford Prison Experiment. The highly controversial experiment was a role-play of sorts, in which college-aged men were assigned to be either guards or prisoners. The experiment had to be stopped after six days because of the abuse the "guards" started inflicting on the "prisoners."

His question was, what makes good people do bad things? In his book, he also observed the behavior of people during Hitler's regime, how untrained German villagers became effective at gathering, torturing, and hunting Jews without any formal training or specific orders. This inner capacity for evil transcends gender, race, and culture.

In his research, Zimbardo also warns against groupthink. Humans succumb to going along with their peers even when they know something is wrong. Numerous social experiments have shown the power of peer pressure to convince people of almost anything, even of things they know are not true. In the face of peer pressure, it's hard to stand up for truth.

When you believe that everyone has a capacity for inflicting suffering, you want to ensure that no one has power to usurp, to hold power unchecked. Government by its nature gives powers to bureaucrats. Our elected representatives often choose to increase that power rather than reduce it or implement processes and incentives that could fuel accountability and effectiveness.

---

13 For more on StrengthsFinder, read *Now Discover Your Strengths* by Marcus Buckingham and Donald Clifton.

In China, the government has access to personal data and can grant or remove rights to buy plane tickets, for instance, based on what is called "social credit."[14]

When we talk about this in Policy Circle discussions, some assume that those in charge will always act in the public's best interest. They want to believe that rules, regulations, and power will be wielded by people who will do the right thing. Surely, they would not abuse power. But we must ask an important question when we give anyone control: what if my worst enemy had this control?

Checks and Balances

In the current climate, there is distrust in "big business." We admire scrappy start-ups, innovative people who come up with a new idea. But when that idea succeeds and the start-up becomes big, growing and hiring and expanding influence, they seem to become "evil." Think of Starbucks, Facebook, Google, Wal-Mart.

In private enterprise, there is an element of self-correction that provides a certain check and balance against the negative traits of human nature. The control is the bottom line and rules of operations. With transparency, the market ultimately corrects for companies that behave unethically or against the best interest of its customers. Competition allows for bad agents to be eliminated on their own: if a company mistreats its employees, those employees will leave or will produce a lower quality service or product, and customers will respond by going to another company. If a company does not provide good service, customers will take their money elsewhere. If there is no competition, the mistreatment can continue, and the bad service or bad product can continue.

In contrast, government agencies face no competition and are often funded through automatic budget processes. The challenge for us as citizens is to ask for policies that eliminate duplications and foster impact, accountability, transparency and efficiencies in government agencies that serve the people and enterprise. The goal of government in a free society is to protect its citizens and unleash human creativity for the greater good.

---

14 https://www.scmp.com/economy/china-economy/article/3096090/
what-chinas-social-credit-system-and-why-it-controversial

Self-Awareness

One of the most disconcerting things about acknowledging the laws of human nature is admitting that you, too, are human. It's one thing to say that humans have weaknesses or the capacity for evil. It's another to see it in yourself. And yet, being aware of both your strengths and your blind spots is essential in the journey toward discovering and using your voice. Sometimes, it means being kind to yourself when you notice a weakness or something you struggle with. That self-awareness is often the first step toward overcoming challenges.

When I was in college, I was in therapy for a while. During a meeting with the school psychologist, I told him that in the course of my studies, I often had to speak in front of a group. The prospect terrified me. In my head, my self-talk was self-defeating! In our group meetings, my thoughts ran something like this: *I'm so nervous to speak up and say an idea. I'm worried so much about how I'm going to say something.* I admitted this to the psychologist. What he told me changed my life in many ways. When I felt that nervousness, he told me to simply become aware of it. Notice my own self-talk. He told me to tell myself, "Oh, here I go again. I'm nervous about speaking up. Here I go again."

He encouraged me to label it, without judging myself, and then move on. Because once you label an emotion, you can just say, "Oh, here I go again, nervous about speaking up." And that kind of takes you outside of the situation, as if you are observing yourself. Astonishingly, this awareness made it easier to speak in front of a group.

This kind of thinking is called meta-thinking. It's thinking about your thinking. And meta-thinking can help us when we have a confidence gap. We just notice our own thinking or feeling, step outside of it, and say, "Oh, look, I'm feeling scared to say something." You might even tell yourself, "Oh, look at me, I'm scared. But I'm going to do it again. I'm going to speak up in spite of the fact I'm scared." Or even, "Wow, I'm being really sarcastic and mean because I feel threatened. I'm going to try to find a way to speak my truth in a firm but kind way." And then, you can decide to be kind to yourself and reassure yourself. Then we can become more objective, step outside of ourselves, and change our self-talk. That kind of self-awareness can be huge. When you become aware of the patterns, you are on the road to change for the better. So, it's not a subconscious pattern anymore, rather, it becomes a conscious thing that you can then overcome.

This is what Susan Packard, author of *Fully Human,* calls emotional fitness. First, you have to be willing to know yourself in order to be able to trust others, feel loved, feel secure, and have compassion for others. When you know yourself, you can achieve peace of mind. When you feel in control, you won't feel afraid. There's a paradox here: When you realize you can't control others, only yourself, it might seem frightening. But it's actually freeing. Once you know yourself, you can encourage and inspire others to do the same, and that's the greatest gift.

If you do not acknowledge the flaws of human nature, you will have a utopian view of the world—that people only do good, only try their best, and always work hard. But the reality is that people are flawed and will often take the path of least resistance. Many don't want to work hard. Few will have this inner motivation to constantly improve, grow, create, innovate.

The question is, how can you overcome that inertia and be the type of person who has that motivation? I think change begins to happen when we know ourselves well enough to be realistic but also to speak our minds. When we share our thoughts, when we use our voice, we begin to change. I've seen it happen time and again in The Policy Circle.

For example, one of the circles in Illinois, the Laurel Circle, discussed civic engagement. They wanted to give back to the community. They chose to cook meals for parents of sick children at Lurie Children's Hospital. This hospital in Chicago is one of the top children's hospitals in the United States, and as a result, they get young patients from around the country who are facing critical illness. Cooking meals gave the circle members a way to overcome hopelessness. It would be easy to go, "There's nothing I can do. It's terrible that children get so sick." This group chose to light a candle instead of cursing the darkness.

Their small but profound act of kindness made a difference not only for those families but also for the women themselves. They experienced the joy of being a difference maker and sparked hope in themselves and others that the world is not all bad.

The group also illustrated a key part of human nature: It is easier to do good with a group. When the circle took on this task, they realized it would not be easy. It meant shopping for food and cooking meals for 55 people! But together, they could do what none of them could do alone. Imagine providing meals for 55 people by yourself! You'd likely say it was too much and give up. But when you join others to speak up, to do good, or both, you're empowered by the strength of the group. Each person brings unique strengths and together you can accomplish a lot!

But how do you even know your strengths are? I've used a number of self-assessment tools to try to understand myself because that helps me to know both my strengths and weaknesses. When I did the StrengthsFinder test, I scored low on harmony, communication, empathy, and competition. That was consistent with my DiSC results, where I am a D (for Dominant, those who focus on results) and C (Conscientiousness, someone who is focused on quality and analysis). I'm not an Influencer (who values relationships) or S (for steady, those who thrive on well defined process and routine).[15] In Enneagram, I'm a Reformer and Challenger.

In other words, I can be hard on people, and that's been the story of my life. I'm in between an introvert and extrovert. I appear to be an extrovert, but I need to withdraw to recharge. How about you? How much do you know about yourself—how your mind works, how you interact with others, what you can achieve? These types of tests are easily accessible, and their insights can provide a key step of growth.

Given that my weakness is people skills, I surround myself with people whose strengths are people skills, process, and details. I appreciate and value them. Truth be told, this was not always the case. I used to have trouble dealing with people who were not like me and pushed them away. Leading The Policy Circle has opened me up to seeing my weaknesses and reaching out to build a team that helps everyone on it, including myself.

While we all tend to ask, "Why can't you be normal like me?" the reality is, we need people who have different strengths than we do. In fact, we should seek them out as mentors, which is what we will talk about in the next chapter.

---

15 Learn more about the DiSC personality test at www.discprofile.com

Trust Challenge:

Read through the 10 features of human nature again. What was your initial response to this list? How have you seen these features play out in your own experience? Have you taken a StrengthFinder, the DiSC, or the Living Languages tests to know yourself?

Have you ever found yourself engaging in self-talk that is self-defeating? This week, pause a few times a day to engage in meta-thinking: noticing your own thinking. Try the techniques suggested to change your negative thoughts into positive ones.

Chapter 3

Trust That You Are Building Something Bigger Than You

As soon as we started The Policy Circle, we found there were plenty of people who had ideas about what it should be. We received many unsolicited suggestions: we should endorse candidates; we should pick issues to advocate. Whether we wanted it or not, everyone had advice.

We had to be very intentional about not letting opinions of others drive our actions. Many of the ideas they offered up didn't align with our vision. We wanted to give women a framework to grow in knowledge and autonomy in their local engagement. The model we chose allows participants to explore their response to the issues we presented. Instead of having invited speakers, we let everyone speak up. We didn't tell them what to do with the information, so the outcomes just naturally came about, in ways that we could not imagine. This was new and different.

When you take risks, try new things, you'll get pushback. I was a bit surprised at the resistance we got for simply doing things a new way. We flipped the model for conversations about policy, and people didn't know what to do. Especially because it was women, there were plenty of critics. It was almost funny: we started something new and innovative, and suddenly, everyone wanted to tell us how to do it—which was the same way it had always been done. Often, people excited about your project will start every sentence with "you should," which should be a red flag. Whether you are starting a company or just engaging in a new project at home or work, be cautious when you hear "you should" because it usually means that this advice comes with no offer to assist in actually getting things done.

While I wanted to be open to new ideas and input, I also did not want to let others, especially those telling me about "the way it had always been done," steer the ship. I listened, but I realized that allowing women a place to discover their voice was something I valued. Trusting my own voice meant valuing the voices of others, so I persisted. I listened to the women who were part of The Policy Circle, but carefully filtered and sometimes chose to ignore people who simply stood outside the organization and tried to change or critique it.

I believe that everyone will have something constructive to say if they truly become informed by the facts. In most groups that discuss policy, the typical way of doing things is speaker-based. You select the speaker who is coming. You know their background and what angle they will bring. You have a lot of control over the message. There is a program, with limited interaction between all the participants.. While this is the way it's often been done, the downside is, it's one-way communication. Study after study shows that most people don't learn or retain as much when they are simply listening to a lecture. When they discuss and wrestle with the ideas and have to formulate their own thoughts, they stretch and grow their minds and ideas.

The Policy Circle allows everyone to read a Policy Circle brief and then speak and share their opinion of it. We let the conversation evolve by allowing everyone to speak and encouraging everyone to listen. Our model challenges the traditional way of talking about policy by giving more people a voice.

With this structure, opinions on policy are going to come out. If members have read the brief and are responding to it, it may evoke something in them. And each person shares the lens through which they experience and understand a policy issue. In fact, that's what makes the conversation productive. By that I mean that people begin to learn from each other and to get clarity about their own opinions and passions. Each person takes the input of the policy brief and holds it up to the light of their own experience and learns from others.

The purpose of The Policy Circle is not to dictate what issue women should advocate for. Instead, we want to help women grow in knowledge, start to see the connections between government, business, citizens, and nonprofits, and see how they can play a role. Seeing how you fit into the bigger picture of enhancing lives is the key to having a growth mindset, loving an industry. When you see your place in the world, you can begin to see yourself reaching a high level of influence and power to achieve your goals.

What Are You Building?

I've heard different versions of an old story, but it basically goes like this:

A woman visits a construction site and sees three laborers working with bricks. She asks each what they are doing. The first says, "I'm laying bricks. I have to finish this pile. Then I get a coffee break." The second says, "I'm constructing a wall. It's going to be a beautiful wall." But the third says, "I'm building a cathedral!"

All three are doing the same job, but the first sees it as just that—a job. The second has a bit more vision, but still doesn't see how his work fits into the work of others. But the third sees the bigger picture, the grander purpose. The third is inspired. He may appear to be doing the same thing that the other two are doing, but he experiences it quite differently, and his impact is therefore far more significant.

Part of trusting your voice is trusting that you are part of a team that is building a cathedral. You're building something bigger than just you. Each of us needs to open our eyes and see the cathedral we are building, and who we are building it with. It may not be obvious to you at first. You need to examine the larger context of what you're doing in every circle of life—individuals, families, communities, cities and nations. Who is building this cathedral with you? You need them, and they need you.

If you've ever visited ancient cathedrals in Europe, you learned that many took decades or even longer to build. The workers who began building them might never have seen the completed cathedral. And yet, they continued. They saw their work as significant and important. When you think of your job, your role in your community, pause and reflect on what grander purpose you are serving. Can you see that your daily tasks are actually part of something bigger? What does that cathedral look like?

The Policy Circle is a place where women can pause and be reminded that each of them is also building a cathedral, and the only way to do it is to work together. As they share their perspective, learn to strengthen their voice, they figure out what cause they care deeply about and want to take action upon.

As I look back at my career, I discover certain themes. Every time I got off track or took missteps, it was because I missed seeing that my job, my role, was serving a grander purpose. In my first job at Accenture, I was thrilled to join an international consulting firm. In my mind, I imagined myself traveling the world working on challenging projects. But as I said earlier, my first assignment was right in my hometown with Canada Post, building an "inventory management system." I was not inspired by my work. All I wanted to do was leave my hometown. Being bilingual, it seemed, was not my ticket out, but my ticket back home.

What I missed seeing is that postal communication is actually the backbone of a country's economy and high-trust societies. The team I was part of worked in Europe, Asia, and the United States.

Instead of seeing the broader possibilities, all I could think of was how much I wanted to leave that project. I also missed seeing the great career growth opportunities I could have had by staying with my team.

If I could go back and tell my younger self a few things, one would be this: Raise your gaze, connect the dots and see the cathedral, the forest through the trees. And notice that no one ever built a cathedral by herself.

Never Alone

"It's better to give before you receive. And never keep score. If your interactions are ruled by generosity, your rewards will follow suit," writes Keith Ferrazzi in his book, *Never Eat Alone.* His book offers business advice on networking and connecting. "Being a connector is not about managing transactions, but about managing relationships," he writes. "The currency of real networking is not greed but generosity."[16] How can you be more

16 Ferrazzi, Keith. *Never Eat Alone: And Other Secrets to Success, One Relationship At A Time.* New York: Crown Business. 2014. p. 22, 8.

generous in your networking? How does giving to others help you to trust your own voice and be sure it is heard?

Americans strive to be completely self-reliant. Sometimes we miss listening to others and seeing the team we are part of. Growth comes when we accept the help of others, and when we, in turn, offer assistance, guidance, and direction to others. That is why both being a mentor and seeking out mentors is an essential part of finding your voice.

Voice feels like it ought to be individualistic, but we often discover our true voice in the context of community. I've seen it happen in The Policy Circle again and again. Women join a circle, and they not only express their opinions (maybe for the first time!) to a group of their peers, but they also develop deeper connections. They find commonality, they find mentors and allies, and they gain the confidence to become mentors to others. They also learn to lead higher-level conversations to shed the veil and discover the cathedral that they are building. Being a mentor is about helping others see the big picture, the forest through the trees, the bird's eye view of the land.

As you seek to discover the cathedral that you are building and map out the roles that you want to play, you will realize that you can't do it alone. You need people to give you advice, people to advocate for you, and people to cheer you on. By that I don't mean someone who just cheers "You can do it!" but doesn't engage beyond that. We all need people who are willing to offer advice, introductions, and recommendations, people who are willing to gently steer us back on track when we need it.

Seek out mentors. Pay attention to the people around you—in your job, in your neighborhood, in whatever context you find yourself. Being part of a Policy Circle, we learn to engage in meaningful conversations, which in turn lets us learn more about people and how we can help each other achieve our goals. Look for someone who is a few steps ahead of you or has an outlook on life that inspires you.

Finding the right mentor begins with self-awareness. In your community, company, or organization, you have to ask yourself a number of questions. The first, really, is "Where do I want to go from here?" What is your purpose, your direction? Engaging with a mentor who is going in a different direction isn't that helpful. Our initial instinct may be to move laterally to develop a set of skills. But why not consider moving up by relying on and continuing to develop effective leadership skills that inspire others?

If you determine where you want to go, then you can look for influencers who are a step ahead of you on the path.

Next, ask yourself, "Who are the influencers? Who has forged the path that I want to take? Who can be encouraging, open doors and help me build relationships, who can help me see the meaning and impact of my role and aspirations?" Determining the answer to these questions requires you to be observant, and one of the best ways to observe is simply to listen to people. Pay attention. Notice who gets things done and who has the most influence. Notice who seems to have that old-fashioned but increasingly rare character trait, wisdom. Pay attention to how various people interact—who is someone who displays emotional intelligence? Don't look for someone who is perfect. Instead, look for someone whose strengths lie in an area you'd like to grow in.

Now, you might expect that I am going to tell you to ask that person to mentor you. But I don't believe that is the best first step.

Offer to Help
Rather than seeking to take from someone, or talk them into mentoring you, change your perspective. Instead, pay attention. What does that person need? How could you help them? Because noticing the needs of others and offering help to them is how you build trust and relationships.

Richard Ryffel, an executive in financial services, has connected many of his colleagues and friends with The Policy Circle. "I consider myself a connector. I like meeting people, and I like solving problems for people. A great way to solve a problem for somebody is to introduce them to some knowledge, or to another person who shares their interest," he said.

When you adopt a servant mindset and seek to help others doors open and the individuals who cross your path help you advance your goal. A few years ago, The Policy Circle team and I attended the Global Leadership Summit, a large leadership conference held at Willow Creek Church in the Chicago suburbs. We just happened to be sitting next to Kathryn Tack and Diane Paddison, leaders and founder of 4word, a women's ministry organization.

Kathryn shared her vision for an engaging C-level forum in Chicago and wanted to create a unique retreat experience. Without hesitation, I offered to facilitate an experience at Wrigley Field.

You always need to figure out a way to help someone achieve their goal. You need to ask, "What are they trying to achieve, and what do I have that can help them do that?" Sometimes, you have to think outside of the box. You may offer a new way of looking at the skills that they have to offer an industry (for instance, a sport historian may be able to offer an innovative way to engage today's baseball fans), or sharing a process that works for you like color coding activities on your calendar based how much they drain or recharge you, or you may have a space, a talent, a connection that adds tremendous value.

Kathryn was delighted with my offer, and so we took the women to a Cubs game, which was really fun. It allowed people to get to know each other in a relaxed setting. And as a result, I was not only a participant in the retreat, but a presenter. I gave a talk about The Policy Circle. I helped Kathryn make the retreat experience memorable, met some amazing and influential women, and had the wonderful opportunity to tell them about my organization. It was a win for all involved. This became the beginning of a personal friendship and on-going collaboration between our organizations.

To offer to help, you have to trust yourself. Even if this person seems to have more experience or operates in a completely different field, you still might be able to offer them something that will help them achieve their goals. And that will build a relationship. You're building a cathedral and you need a team of people to help you do it.

Author Sam Adeyemi writes: "There is tremendous power in mentoring that transforms you into the kind of person your mentor is. The result of mentoring is not just information; it is formation. Anyone who can influence your thinking can influence your life . . . Mentors stretch your mind."[17]

---

17 Adeyemi, Sam. *Success Is Who You Are.* p. 98.

The Confidence Gap

As I look at my own career path and listen to women who have become a part of The Policy Circle, I notice a gap—a confidence gap. There's a chasm between what they think they can do and what they can actually do and. In other words, they are capable of more than they give themselves credit for. It's a confidence gap.

I believe that's why there is sometimes a hesitation to embrace the structure of The Policy Circle. They're unsure of themselves, so they want an expert, a speaker, a teacher—someone who can give them all the facts. But more facts are not going to give them the confidence they seek. Confidence is not just one thing; it is built with a multitude of small wins. Confidence is like a fabric, woven of many threads—positive experiences, support of others, even our mistakes and what we learn from them.

When we started The Policy Circle, the women who attended didn't trust themselves to discuss a topic that they were unfamiliar with. The stated purpose and structure was to simply read the brief and discuss it. But somehow, even deciding to take the time to read about a new topic can be daunting and intimidating.

But when they actually read the brief, participated in a roundtable discussion, and realized they did have ideas, opinions, and questions—wow, it was a powerful experience that ignited a new confidence, meaningful connections and a sense of power to influence.

We were doing something new and lots of people challenged the idea. Which is great, because challenges and competition makes what we do better as long as we stay focused. If I'm nervous about what I'm doing, I use that little phrase, "Here I go again" to kind of take myself outside of the emotions. By doing so, I'm showing compassion to myself. And reminding myself, I don't stop or give up just because I'm a little nervous or people are critical.

Being part of a Policy Circle can be transformative as we expand our knowledge and ecosystem of relationships. I think, for example, of my friend Stacey. A former CPA, she'd had a career in finance but then took a break to raise her children for about 10 years. She was part of the very first Policy Circle meetings. She became more aware of state and local policy issues. In 2016, her neighbors encouraged her to run for office, a local township board.

In order to run for office, she had to update her LinkedIn profile, and participated in some debates and presentations for candidacy. Someone who was on the state pension investment board took notice of her. This person nominated Stacey to be on the board because he looked at her background. After meeting her and hearing her speak to a group, he felt like she could be a person that would bring people together toward making decisions.

Stacey accepted the nomination, and throughout the nomination process she had the opportunity to go to conferences and broaden her network. This gave her confidence, but there was still a gap. We met for coffee, and she told me she was thinking about going back to full-time work in finance. She had decided that she could pursue a career in institutional financial advising. So, she told me, "I'm going to talk to this guy and see if I could work in his company. I'm even willing to work at a lower level just so I can learn the business."

I looked at her and told her, "No, you are not going to do that."

She looked extremely surprised.

"You have a lot of experience," I told her. "You have a lot to bring, and so you should not say that you're willing to start at entry level or anything like that. Do not use those words."

So many women are willing to work at a lower level than they're worth—especially if they have been out of the marketplace for a while to care for their family. We have to learn to ask for what we're worth. The confidence gap keeps us from doing that.

Stacey ended up going back to work. Being a part of The Policy Circle led her path back to work and helped her get noticed because it gave her the confidence to step out of her comfort zone. She also started a Policy Circle with other women in finance.

Spheres of Care
While you have to remember you are building a cathedral, you are not building *every* cathedral. You cannot do everything and manage everyone.

You play a role that matters in the larger scheme of things, but you have to be aware of your sphere of care.

In their book *Breaking Through Gridlock,* Jason Jay and Gabriel Grant offer a helpful framework, which we use a lot in The Policy Circle. Everyone has a sphere of care. It begins at the center of a circle, with yourself. We all have some level of self-interest and self-preservation. We care about what happens to us. We watch out for our own interests, and that is healthy.

Beyond ourselves, the spheres of care extend in concentric circles. Immediately outside of ourselves are our interpersonal relationships. This could include our family, friends, neighbors, and other people we know.

Beyond that, we care also about larger spheres, where we may not know everyone but of which we're a part. Those spheres, radiating outward, include the following: community (which might also be your business or organization), nation (which could be your country, or your "people"), humanity, and all beings.

When addressing an issue or figuring out the bigger picture, it's important to know how to articulate your sphere of care. The sphere of care will impact how you react to any problem or situation you face. It is a powerful tool to understand other people's point of view and your own.

This is a useful image to share the lens through which you analyze a situation, ideas, policies. Your sphere of care may be different based on the issue or it may be very consistent. For instance, your first reaction may always be to care for your family, your business or profession. I've noticed that my first reaction is always to care for humanity. I transpose a problem to the world, or to a bigger scale, when actually the biggest impact is local and starts with your own family or community.

For instance, when I look at the complex issue of immigration, I think about the bigger picture—how will immigration impact our country on a large scale? The individuals involved are suffering; this is true. For many different reasons, they may feel that their only choice is to pay smugglers to illegally cross the border. That choice has consequences, not just for them but for the country they are trying to enter. Nations need to know who lives within their borders, and people who live within the borders need to contribute to education, health, infrastructure, and security.

Many immigrants come to the U.S. legally on a work or school visa, then overstay that visa, becoming undocumented. In fact, 42 percent of undocumented immigrants are those who've overstayed a legal visa.[18] Others come to the border and present themselves to border officials to request asylum, which is legal. However, the problem of what to do with these asylum seekers while their case is pending is the source of plenty of disagreement. Immigration policy is complicated, but identifying your sphere of care may help you sort out which policies you support.

I cannot go to England and choose to stay and work there, I will be deported.

My sphere of care is the nation. In discussions on immigration, some of my friends are close to people crossing the borders and their suffering— their sphere of care is individual humans. Many immigrants are fleeing terrible conditions in other countries. Should we help try to stabilize those countries, so people don't have to uproot themselves? If so, how? What if the governments in those countries don't want our "help"?

Awareness of each person's sphere of care helps you to see other people's perspective without judging it. The sphere of care makes you realize that everyone is in a different sphere based on time, and personal experience. If you can articulate your sphere of care, you are at peace with your thoughts, you can acknowledge other perspectives and you can start finding solutions.

When we started The Policy Circle, we were learning how to onboard individual circle leaders. One of our first circle leaders, Lisa, was responsible for helping women start new circles. She was reaching out to them individually, building connections, understanding their hesitations and answering questions. It takes courage to convene a group for discussion on broad topics such as poverty, government regulations, economic growth, foreign policy and trade, and human topics such as aging, mental health, or the Fabric of Neighborhood. Lisa's focus and sphere of care was the individual circle leaders. My co-founder Angela Braly, who serves on the board of several large companies, pushed us to always keep in mind scalability. What would this process look like with 10,000 circle leaders globally? Her sphere of care is at a larger level.

---

18 See http://bit.ly/3c9RTx3

This concept of sphere of care allows us to understand differences in perspectives, but also allows us to grow, to move forward. We have to remember that as we build a cathedral, we need people with different perspectives on our team. We need to work with people who might disagree with us. Our differences, though, are often a matter of where each of us tends to focus.

Horizon of Care

In Policy Circle discussions, I have noticed that another area where people misunderstand each other is the horizon of care. This has to do with time—immediate, midterm, long term. In the current debate on immigration, for example, people are quick to jump to conclusions on others' perspectives. Some people care about alleviating human suffering immediately, like attending to the immediate needs of undocumented immigrants caught at the border living in temporary facilities, for example. Others might worry about the long-term implications and sustainability of accepting/caring for illegal immigrants, and the criminal activity of some smugglers. There is also the case of accepting refugees of political crises immediately vs. first questioning the role of U.S. foreign policy to improve the conditions of life in other countries so that people can stay and live a good life.

In business, everyone needs to agree on the time horizon that decisions will impact: immediate (up to three months), midterm (one to two years), or long lasting change. We may set 10-year goals and vision, and then three-year goals that if achieved will get us there. Those three-year goals are broken down into this year goals and quarterly rocks that will give us focus.[19]

At The Policy Circle, we want activities that will fuel a steady growth of circles that we can support adequately, however, in three years we want to triple the number of circles. So those goals drive decision-making and investment priorities, for instance, in marketing or new technology.

A company may choose to acknowledge that work-life balance is not an immediate need to be addressed to care for new mothers, but rather, a long-term issue for all workers as they are called to care not only for children but also aging parents. A long-term scope changes the framing of policy.

---

19 The book *Traction: Get a Grip on Your Business* by Gino Wickman offers an excellent model for goal-setting that is easy to implement.

Another example might be the issue of parity on boards. How can we get women on corporate boards, getting them a seat at the table, so to speak? Some people believe we should work for legislation that would force companies to have women on their boards, thinking that will fix the problem once and for all. However, with regulations comes monitoring, which means additional costs, inspections, and forms to fill—another burden on businesses. A mandatory requirement diminishes the value and qualifications of the appointee. Research suggests "that shifting the diversity discourse away from gender to other dimensions of expertise and experience might, in fact, help women and other underrepresented groups – for example, instead of saying 'we have appointed a female director' the focus should be 'we have appointed an expert on China.' With less emphasis on gender, female appointments might one day no longer be perceived as checking a social performance box, and signal nothing about firm preferences other than its commitment to hiring the best people for the job."[20]

How does this relate to knowing yourself, to trusting your voice? In my opinion, each of us has a propensity to operate in one part of the time horizon or another. It is helpful to know your own propensity so you can understand others.

Living Your Values
As you build your cathedral, it's important to not only be aware of your spheres of care and horizon of care but also the values that drive your decisions. Can you articulate your values and principles?

If we are to move forward in using our voice, in building something of meaning, be it in our career, our family, or our community—we must be intentional about making decisions based on our values. Do you know what your values are? What is important to you? These need to be things that impact your actions, not just your ideas. What do you value and put into practice?

When I thought about this for myself, I came up with the following list. This is who I am and how we operate in our family.

20 **Isabelle Solal** is a postdoctoral research fellow at the James M. and Cathleen D. Stone Centre for the Study of Wealth Inequality at INSEAD, https://hbr.org/2019/11/why-investors-react-negatively-to-companies-that-put-women-on-their-boards

- **Walk the talk**. I believe that if you say you value something, your actions should reflect it. One area where I try to live out my values is in caring for the environment. I care about clean water, clean air, and less waste. I have been using reusable bags since 1994. I made my own baby food back in 2002. I bike in town and to the market. When my children were small, I would carry all three of them on my Xtracycle cargo bike. I compost. I value the environment and protecting it, and I believe my small actions make a difference. I don't impose on others what I don't do myself.

  Another area where I live authentically is in leadership. At The Policy Circle, all team members must also be circle leaders so we can live the life of the circle leader, use the website, and discuss the briefs. We encourage women to get engaged in the public policy dialogue and the political process, so I do that as well.

- **Value personal autonomy.** I value choice and letting people decide what works for them and their circumstances.

- **Live with an abundance mentality.** I learned this idea from one of Stephen Covey's early books, *Principle-Centered Leadership*. Instead of the hoarding that a scarcity mentality fosters, an abundance mentality keeps you open. If you think that there is enough for everyone, you will embrace collaboration, applaud good ideas, and think, "Imitation is the greatest compliment."

- **Elevate and be world class.** In our family and with the Policy Circle, we believe that details matter. We don't cut corners, and we strive to offer the best experience. We elevate the conversation instead of keeping it in the gutter. At The Policy Circle, we started small, but my co-founders really pushed us to not think small, to not feel small, to punch higher. This also means looking for best practices when solving processes. Looking for best practices all the time, everywhere and from anyone.

- **No labels**. The human brain makes sense of the world by categorizing and stamping labels. But labels are too simple to capture our multifaceted lives. It reduces a person to one dimension, when in actuality we are multidimensional, we wear many hats, and our heart and mind are shaped by our life experiences.

Focusing on the common goal and the many ways to get there—instead of labeling—unlocks innovation and builds trust.

- **Be a life enhancer.** I constantly work to solve problems—I see a situation and I want to fix it long term (not Band-Aid it, really fix it). That means that when I take a ball, I don't drop it until it's fixed. The Policy Circle has embraced this internal principle to the point where everyone feels like they own issues and collaborate to fix them instead of throwing them over the fence. On a personal level, I try to not pick up new balls. I don't need to fix everything. As Mother Theresa said, "Never worry about numbers. Help one person at a time, and always start with the person nearest you."

Keeping your own values front and center will help you to align your actions with your purpose. It will remind you not just that you are building a cathedral, but it will shape the specific cathedral that you've been given to build. As you live your values, you'll begin to build trust. You'll trust that your words and impact really do matter. That is what we'll explore in the next chapter.

Trust Challenge:

Think about the primary focus of your life. In broader terms, what are you contributing to build?

Make a list of five of your most deeply held values. Then add specific things you are doing, or want to do, to live out these values.

Chapter 4

Trust That Your Voice
Will Spark Others

Your voice matters. Your words have power. Your impact, even if you can't see it right away, sends out a spark that becomes a flame that can change other people's lives—for better or worse. When you see the gift that your own voice is, you realize that you can be a spark to others—you can ignite something in them that perhaps they never imagined. You can inspire them to do something they never would otherwise have done.

For example, Amanda and Lindsay co-lead a circle in Fort Wayne, Indiana. Being a part of The Policy Circle inspired both to get involved politically. When Lindsay decided to run for city council, it sparked an idea in Amanda. She became the campaign manager for Lindsay's campaign. Never having run a campaign before, she started doing her research and jumped into volunteering on other local campaigns to gain more experience.

Amanda gained a valuable new mentor, State Senator Justin Busch, who took her under his wing and taught her more about campaigns and strategies. Things snowballed somewhat organically after that. Amanda's newfound passion for being an expert on local campaigns led her to become even more involved. She became precinct committeewoman and state delegate for the Allen County Republican Party, as well as a grassroots director for Senator Busch's 2020 campaign.

Amanda was also one of 15 women in Indiana selected for the Richard G. Lugar Excellence in Public Service Series, a leadership training experience that "encourages, mentors and prepares selected women leaders across Indiana to seek new levels of personal achievement and public involvement."[21]

"The Policy Circle discussions bring to the table that common understanding is what is needed to bridge the divides we have now," Amanda says. She sees the support and camaraderie from fellow circle members as the biggest benefit of Policy Circle membership.

Amanda's story is one of many. The Policy Circle sparked a passion in her and taught her to trust her voice.

Finding Meaning

By the time I got to college, I was an atheist, or maybe you could call it agnostic. I didn't really believe anything. It all seemed unknowable.

I worked hard, but there were many times when I wondered what my hard work was for. What was the point? This sometimes led me down a dark path. I sometimes felt despondent, or that life was meaningless. I assumed that everyone had similar thoughts and feelings.

I grew up Catholic, but that mostly meant following rituals and just enduring the pain of life until you got rewarded somehow in heaven for your suffering. So, I didn't embrace that tradition as faith, and certainly didn't make it my own. The problem with being an atheist is that you feel really alone. You don't have a framework of beliefs, or a supportive community, to give your life purpose and meaning because you are part of a bigger plan. Looking back now, I can see it would have been good to have that kind of faith framework, I think.

It used to be that when people would talk about faith or God, my line was always, "What does God have against Africa?" Really, that was my way of asking, Why do some good people seem to suffer so much? How could a good God allow suffering and pain and genocide? It's a question a lot of

---

21 Learn more at https://lugarseries.com/

people use to keep from even considering spiritual things. And I did not see the truth. And now I look back and realize that my life would have been different if I had had some kind of faith. I doubt it would have been as hard in terms of stress. It's stressful to think that life doesn't have a bigger meaning.

It was also overwhelming to move to the United States for my post-graduate work. When I first came here, my English was not very good. I was at this top university working toward a master's in computer science, yet everyone else felt smarter, more academic. I'm technical. I wasn't a genius, so attending a top-tier university, I felt out of place. I didn't understand what people were saying sometimes. I had to write down all the words that I didn't understand to perfect my English.

In my mid-twenties, I was curious about all different religions. I traveled to India and stayed for a retreat in a Tibetan monastery near Dharamsala, where I made a promise to return or to experience a retreat on a regular basis. I wondered about spirituality, but I didn't understand it. Faith was both fascinating and mysterious to me. But I set aside those questions when I didn't find immediate answers. I didn't know then that later in life, they'd resurface at just the right time, when I encountered other people who could reignite my spiritual curiosity.

In that season of my life, I did not see that I was building a cathedral. I was just in survival mode—as are many young women who are juggling a family and career. I did not see the larger meaning, how my impact on others could actually give my life a feeling of significance and meaning.

I was afraid of failure. But failing is learning, and it happens to all of us. I recently heard Gail Boudreau, CEO of Anthem, speak at a lunch for The Chicago Network. "Be curious," she said. "Don't be afraid to fail. Raise your hand. Continue to learn and grow. Try to learn something new all the time."

When you raise your hand, you are not going to have the right answer all of the time. You're going to make mistakes. But by exploring and making mistakes, you also learn, and you find meaning. You discover who you are and how you can impact the world. In other words, by risking and even experiencing failure, you find meaning. Your life becomes more satisfying, even in its imperfection. Your struggles no longer lead you to despair but to deeper insights. Just as Thomas Edison famously said that he had learned 10,000 ways not to make a light bulb, you learn from your mistakes.

When I met Angela Braly at that conference, and she compared my idea of a discussion group on policy to a Bible study, it was something I'd never heard of. But then, things began to happen. I kept meeting people of faith. All kinds of faith: Christian, Muslim, Jewish. And their faith was a part of their life. It seemed to give them meaning.

Not long after we met, Angela invited me to the Global Leadership Summit, which I mentioned in the previous chapter. It was an incredible conference, a gathering of 10,000 people, and they were talking about management and leadership but incorporating their faith into it. They talked about how faith guided them, influenced their decisions, and helped them find answers to problems. I'd never heard that before, and it was really refreshing.

As I mentioned earlier, Diane Paddison and Kathryn Tack, two friends of Angela's, just happened to be sitting near us in this vast auditorium, and that introduction led to me helping Kathryn with her retreat. Diane is the founder of 4word, a national network of professional Christian women. These women of faith have become good friends of mine.

That conference was a huge turning point. For the first time in my life, I encountered professional women who were talking about their faith and incorporating it into their business life, their leadership.

I remembered my retreat in India, my curiosity (and skepticism) about faith. Of course, work, marathons, marriage, and kids took precedence over my spiritual musings. But for some reason, these women became friends, and their influence reawakened some of my curiosity about faith and where it might fit in my life. The way they lived their life, with faith at the center, sparked questions that had been dormant for a long time.

Hearing Diane's story about how women in the church are often not invited to share their professional expertise, whether it is finance or real estate or business, surprised me. I didn't know enough about the Christian subculture to understand how it treated women. But it was in many ways similar to how our culture at large still confines women to specific roles.

In her organization, 4word, Diane had created something similar to The Policy Circle. It was really about bringing people together. It made me realize that you can establish yourself as a civic leader in your community through your faith. Maybe building a new synagogue or being effective in your church—it allows you to be impactful, establishing yourself as a leader in your community. You can invite people to participate more in their faith community.

I'd always thought of religion as a source of conflict between people rather than a source of healing and bringing people together. I did not fully grasp—until we moved to Chicago, started going to church, and sent our kids to Sunday school—what it looked like to be a part of a church. I didn't realize it was a place for forging relationships, for finding a supportive community.

And people's faith is much more active than what you hear in mainstream media and Hollywood. This is an area where I'm still learning and exploring. But in the last few years it's definitely become more a part of my life.

A few years ago, my father-in-law, Joe Ricketts, established a silent Ignatian retreat center in Gretna, Nebraska, called the Cloisters on the Platte. He goes on this type of retreat once a year, and it was his experiences on those retreats in other locations that inspired him to establish this retreat center. It opened in 2019, a magnificent location to retreat in silence for three days. Ignatian retreats[22] are a chance to get away from distractions of modern life and spend time mostly in silent reflection, focusing on God rather than our busy lives. It's a chance to set aside distractions, spend time in solitude and silence, and simply be still.

I have the opportunity to go on an annual retreat at Cloisters on the Platte, remembering my promise years before to make time for this spiritual practice.

"It is Better to Speak"

You can be a spark, igniting others to make a difference or to see things in a new way. You can bring about change, but it begins with yourself. Your voice matters. Your impact, your opinion, your actions—these things make

---

22 Cloisters on the Platte https://cloistersontheplatte.com/make-a-retreat/ ignatian-practices/

a difference. One of the best things that The Policy Circle has done for me is to remind me how much every voice matters. By providing a place for women to share their ideas, and helping them grow in confidence, I became more confident myself.

If we don't speak up, don't ask our questions, then our curiosity does nothing for us or for others. We have to be willing to trust our own voice and ideas and questions enough to put them out there. To be bold, even when our voice shakes.

The poet Audre Lorde once said, "When we speak we are afraid our words will not be heard or welcomed. But when we are silent, we are still afraid. So it is better to speak."

By learning about yourself and how much your voice matters, you can be a spark for others. Mentors spark others, helping them to see the gift that is in each person. How can you be a spark?

You may say to yourself, but how can I mentor others? You may tell yourself, I've made mistakes along the way. You may secretly think, I don't really know what I'm doing. But even the challenges we face can be a gift, teaching us perseverance, grit, and—sometimes—how not to do things!

After I married Todd, I worked at Ameritrade. This was in 2000, and the dot-com bubble was huge—of course, at the time we didn't realize it was a bubble. We thought it was just wonderful growth and opportunity.

A friend of ours secured the domain ecotravel.com, and we had the lovely idea of creating an online business. At that time, this was new and cutting edge; people were figuring out how to use the internet to do business. Ecotourism was a new thing at the time, and we thought we could create a website for promoting it. I was ahead of the curve on ecotourism and all things green: reusable bags, reusable lunch boxes, composting, biking instead of driving. You name it, I was doing it.

So, my husband and I began building ecotravel.com, which was a directory of ecotourism companies. And then, the dot-bomb happened, where advertisements for companies crashed, and then, 9/11 happened. Suddenly, American tourism of all kinds went way down. Especially tourism to other countries. People were afraid, and they certainly didn't want to travel internationally.

Our little dot-com business screeched to a halt. And then, in 2002, I had a baby. We were not sure what our next step was, but an interesting opportunity came along. Todd's dad owned a bison ranch in Wyoming, and we moved out there so that Todd could manage the ranch. We lived on the ranch, which may sound fun, but I found it was more difficult than I expected.

Living in a remote location far from family and friends feels isolating. People would come to visit and enjoy the outdoors, but then they would leave. Back then I did not know how to become part of the fabric of a community. I only knew how to find a community in a big city, through things like running, the arts, the myriad experiences offered in a big city, and of course, the work community.

Suddenly, we were alone with a newborn, far away from everything. The pediatrician's office was an hour away, and just going to the movies was a five-hour trip. Today, with the experience of The Policy Circle, I would actually know how to connect to the community by reading the local paper, understanding the functioning of the local government, and meeting the members of the Chamber of Commerce. I'd know I could visit the local rec center or even organize opportunities to connect with local residents around ideas and local challenges.

Step Out of Your Comfort Zone
We moved back to Chicago, and we returned to professional life. Like most families, we juggled travel calendars (this was before Google calendar, if that can be imagined), metro commutes, daycare, ear infections, and weekend baby activities. I moved from working with software to hardware, and was an executive program manager at Chase, working in technology infrastructure. Looking back, this was actually a big step out of my comfort zone. I had to lean into the relationships that I had made to find a job. I did not question the job. I was grateful for a job in a great bank where I met phenomenal people. I was a woman in technology, but I never thought of myself that way. I was just trying to do the best that I could to deliver on the projects that I was trusted with.

I don't recall any mentoring programs or any special leadership development programs for women. I had joined Bank One, a Chicago-based financial institution that was then acquired by Chase, which in turn was acquired by JP Morgan. The organization that I had originally joined had a swift "get it done" culture that I loved and learned to navigate. However, being absorbed by another organization is hard. Reporting structures change, approach changes, culture changes. I could not see a path for myself, either up or sideways. I felt trapped on a treadmill.

That feeling of being trapped was amplified by coming home and realizing that my daughter was not speaking French to me because I was not there to converse with her. In my family, not having bilingual children would be deemed as a failure in parenting. So, I decided to leave corporate life.

I look back today and think that when there is a will, there is a way. I didn't really explore ways to make things work. I could have asked to work part-time, which might have opened other opportunities in other departments. But I had an all-or-nothing mentality because I just couldn't see that there is always a middle path.

A New Venture

A few years later, one of my husband's college friends called my husband with the idea to invest in a local bike shop whose owner had unfortunately passed away. I wasn't much of a cyclist, but my husband and dad certainly were. My dad was not only into cycling, he was instrumental in getting bike paths built in Quebec. He was the first mayor to bike from our town hall to Quebec City, as part of his campaign to communicate a vision of a network of bike trails connecting cities across the province.

His vision became a reality: La Route Verte has been named by *National Geographic* as "the world's greatest bike trail." It is more than 5,000 kilometers long—the longest cycling path network in North America. In their retirement years, my parents biked all over Europe and Canada.

Owning a retail store is an "all in" kind of thing for the families involved. There's a local Chamber of Commerce, there are weekend rides, citywide events, community groups to join to promote bike trails. I found myself drawn to discovering the biking culture, driving communications with our customers and noticing that women hesitated to buy bikes for themselves. I organized weekly women rides and rode my bike everywhere with kids in tow to inspire others. I went from a novice hesitant to ride with cleats to a "weekend warrior" helping others change a flat tire. In the early 2000s, women biking was emerging; it is exciting to think that I played a part in swelling that wave. It was interesting the number of women who did not feel deserving of a higher-end bike. They would spend the money on outfits, restaurants, and trips but not on a bike. But in biking, as in many sports, the quality of the gear matters.

Jumping into owning a bike shop meant we quickly became part of a larger biking community. We connected with World Bicycle Relief, an amazing organization that provides bikes designed for Africa's rugged terrains to healthcare workers and girls attending remote schools. The bikes provide safe transportation and enable healthcare workers to see more patients because they don't have to walk from village to village.

To promote Cubs Charities and World Bicycle Relief, my husband, Todd, suggested that the two organizations organize a century ride from Wrigley Field in Chicago to Miller Park in Milwaukee. That 100-mile bike ride inspired Cubs fans to bike.

The impact this had was astonishing. For many of us, it was the first time that we had embarked on a 100-mile bike ride. One woman heard about the ride on the news. She decided, right then, she was going to do that 100-mile ride from Wrigley Field to Milwaukee. She didn't even own a bike.

She came to our shop, bought a bike, and started doing the Saturday rides to train for the Wrigley ride. She lost weight and got very fit. She not only completed the ride, she began to really change her life. She eventually became a police officer with the city of Chicago.

Since we're in Chicago, part of the year is too snowy and cold to bike outdoors. So, we set up a CompuTrainer cycling studio in the shop. CompuTrainer measures your effort and cadence. You use it to stay fit and train through the winter. Each person works individually but there are classes where you can ride together. We even became part of a series of races put on by the CompuTrainer. We also organized cyclo-cross races and participated in the Chicago cyclo-cross race series. This brought traffic into the shop during the off-season, and eventually it turned into its own little community of bike riders.

I was part of the success of the shop, but what's odd is that I didn't see it as a real job. I was just helping out. Plenty of women do the same thing: They're an essential partner in a family business, but they label it "just helping out, or being part of the team." I wasn't in the corporate world, and so I didn't think it counted somehow. But I look back at it now and realize my impact mattered. My involvement in promoting biking in the community, and specifically to women, helped the bike shop thrive. But at the time, I didn't see it.

But, even though I didn't see it, I was sparking change, both in people around me and in myself. I was learning about how to connect people, how to organize people around a common cause, how to engage women. Much of what I learned in the work I did there has impacted my leadership of The Policy Circle. What I did at the bike shop helped me to value people who are willing to lead circles today.

Showing Up

My husband and I are fortunate to be part of a large family, a convivial community, and have gathered so many friends throughout our lives. We are therefore invited to a lot of events and gatherings. We care about our friends, and it is hard to say no.

However, I lead toward the introvert side of the spectrum, which means that being with large groups drains me. I need time to regroup and recharge at home, either alone or with just a few friends. Being naturally more shy, I tend to tell myself that showing up to these events doesn't really matter. If it's a big event, no one will notice if I'm not there, right?

I only recently realized that showing up matters to others. Being there and interacting in person is the glue to a community. It is also what makes us feel happy, wholesome, worthwhile.

The word "friend" does not mean what it once did. Facebook, by calling everyone who can spell your name a "friend," has diminished the value of the word. For me, friends are those who will show up when you ask them.

When I turned 25 for the second time, my husband organized a surprise party for me. He didn't just invite our neighbors—he invited good friends from Canada, good friends from Omaha, friends from all over the U.S. People I had not seen in 10 years showed up for my birthday. Even thinking about it now, emotions stir up. It was the first time that I realized the value of showing up. I could not believe that they took the time to travel all that way to celebrate with me. I was so touched. It warmed my heart. I realized that everyone's presence matters, that a note matters, that a call matters.

Be a Spark

What can you do to be a spark, to spark others into action? I am always looking for ways to be a spark. Because it makes life more interesting and fun. It's not hard to do—just pay attention to others and be creative. When you take a risk to initiate, you begin to trust your voice more. You see that your voice can spark others.

A few years ago, I was a part of a local running group made up of friends from my neighborhood, mostly other moms I'd met through my kids' activities and school. We went for runs together, trained for races together, and just enjoyed the camaraderie of running. One of the women in the group, Eleanor, had a birthday in August. She told us how because people are often on vacation in August, she rarely gets to celebrate her birthday with friends.

Hearing that made me wonder—how could I celebrate my friend? I love hosting people for a Cubs game at Wrigley, so I decided it would be fun to combine that with running. The goal was not a cause; it was just something fun and silly for Eleanor and the rest of us.

I said, "You know what? I'll celebrate your birthday! Let's do a 'Run to Wrigley for Eleanor's Birthday.'"

So, I had T-shirts printed up with a drawing of a cake with candles and the words "Running to Wrigley for Eleanor's Birthday." And then we ran to Wrigley from Eleanor's house, which was about 13 miles (the distance for a half marathon). We watched the game and drank Gatorade and ate hot dogs. Everyone had a lot of fun. A few women who had not run with us simply drove to the ballpark. They drove us home so that we didn't have to run another 13 miles after the game!

We kept finding other milestones to celebrate with that special run event. The next one was for one of the moms who'd had at least one child at our local elementary school for 13 years running. So, for her, we created the "13 miles to Wrigley to celebrate the end of 13 years as a Central School mom."

Another year, it was Christy's half birthday, so we decided we would do a "Half Marathon to Wrigley for Christy's half birthday." It was fun. We would just run from the house of the person we were celebrating and go to Wrigley.

What was even funnier was people who would text me saying, "I know you organize the Run to Wrigley. Can I sign up?" I had to explain it wasn't a race or public event. It was just something to spark some fun with my running group. I did it so that it would be fun to keep running—not a real race, not a charity, just a spark to make us smile and connect.

More recently, a conversation with friends helped to spark another idea. We often spend time in Big Sky, Montana. Over the holidays, I was on a snowshoe hike. The other women on the hike and I started talking about organizing a women's weekend. I'd heard about other women's weekends that combine fitness and ideas. I'm excited that as I write this, it is coming together.

The weekend will be a two-day event focusing on fitness and ideas. The goal is to bring together other women from the Big Sky community who love fitness and are interested in discussing ideas that impact us and our communities such as health disparities, impact investing, housing, and the fabric of neighborhoods. One of the women, Ayaan Hirsi Ali, happens to be launching a book, so one of the talks on the agenda is about her book, *Prey: Immigration, Islam, and the Erosion of Women's Rights,* which is about Europe's immigration experience. We have about 20 women from the community attending, and they are so excited. Again, I was able to serve as the catalyst and leverage The Policy Circle model to organize a uniquely enriching experience.

The whole event started with just a conversation. When you hear people say, "Wouldn't it be great if we could..." you have a choice. You can leave it there, in the idea stage, and it won't happen at all. Or, you can wait and hope someone else does something. Or, you can trust that your voice can be a spark to others. You can jump in and decide to not just wish someone else would do something. Instead, you can believe that if you do something, you'll start something exciting that you and others can be a part of.

How can you be a spark? By helping others to see the gift, to ignite something in them that will launch a new project. In my work with women in

The Policy Circle, I found that it takes courage to host a conversation on a substantive topic and it is easy to get bogged down in the tiny details.

Be a spark, not the cold water that puts out the fire! Don't get hung up on the small details. Allow yourself to just see the big pictures and not all of the hurdles.

Believe in Yourself

Often, our biggest hurdle is ourselves. We don't realize our value and worth. While it's normal to doubt our impact, sometimes we just have to step forward. We have to change our thinking and our actions, and the results will follow.

An important first step is self-awareness. Are you a realist focused on measurable outcomes (just the facts), pessimist (looking for reasons something won't work), or an optimist (focused on people's good intentions, even if people don't live up to those intentions)? One way to tell is to notice where you go, how you act, and when you are getting angry (or very annoyed). What stirs up your anger? How can we channel our anger in a positive way, to bring about change in others or ourselves?

The Policy Circle experience has changed the way I interact with people, the way that I see people's focus, passions, superpowers, and potential contributions to the world. In traveling the country to seed Policy Circles, I keep meeting women who underestimate the value of what they do and what they contribute.

In my experience, this is especially true of women in their forties and older. Women who help with a family business, for example (as I did with our bike shop), tend to downplay their role, rather than counting it as an accomplishment or relevant business experience. We've been socially conditioned to not brag about ourselves, but in business, that can easily erode our confidence.

In a conversation with several recruiters in legal, technology and accounting, all agreed that women are often afraid to ask for what they are worth, especially if they have gaps in their resume.

One recruiter said that women will typically only apply for jobs when they know they have at least 80 percent of the skills or experience required.

Men, on the other hand, will confidently apply for jobs where they have about 50 percent.

"Women, if you ask if they have a skill, and they don't, they'll say no," she said. "If you ask a man, 'Have you done X, Y, and Z?' he will say, 'Well, I've done A, B, and C, and that will help me to figure out X, Y and Z.' That's what employers want to hear—that you know how to figure it out."

Recruiters say they do see the trend is changing, as younger women "are more likely to oversell themselves" on their resume and in an interview than older women. They're less afraid to ask for higher compensation.

I have an attorney friend who contributes to the management team of her family business and drives employee volunteer efforts in the community. Yet, she has a blank profile on LinkedIn.

The point is not to get women to brag or oversell themselves. Rather, by realizing the value of our experience and skills, we can help others and ourselves to advance and grow. Using social platforms like LinkedIn allows us to connect, contribute, and exchange. We just need the confidence to believe that we have something unique to contribute, that what we share may inspire others to reach a new level.

The year we started The Policy Circle, we leaned on technology to enable leaders to establish a circle, communicate with their circle members and other circles in their area, and access the library of The Policy Circle briefs. At first, I was doing everything with a friend and volunteer, Lisa, who believed in the model. I was editing briefs, leading expansion, and building the technology with a consulting firm as we grew and realized the functionalities that we needed.

My biggest weakness is impatience. I needed help to define and implement the technology and the processes if we were to grow. In the midst of it all, I somehow found the time to attend a PTA meeting where my friend and fellow mom, Molly, gave a presentation on a project she'd spearheaded, in which she'd migrated the school district's family directories from paper to an app-based directory for all eight schools in the district. As Molly presented the detailed process of this conversion, I told myself, "This is the person I need!"

The next day I called Molly for coffee and convinced her to come on board as a contractor. I saw her ability to gather requirements, plan and execute an implementation, and develop processes to support a new way of doing things—the skills we needed. Molly took on the challenge, learned new technology and new tools, and applied her project-management skills in change management to building communities.

Being a key part of our team sparked something in Molly. And after five years with The Policy Circle, she is being offered positions with startups and established her own consulting firm. Molly was a stay-at-home mom for more than a decade, but now that her boys are college-bound, she is fully back in the workforce, ready for yet another exciting new chapter in which she continues to be financially independent.

Seeing the potential in others is about seeing the connections, the transferability of knowledge, skills, and experiences to a new environment. That's what being a spark is about.

Trust Challenge:

I helped run a business but saw it as "just helping out." Ask yourself, What am I downplaying in what I contribute at work, in my family, as a hobby, or with friends?

What can you do to be a spark, to spark others into action?

In this chapter, we read a quote from the poet Audre Lorde: "When we speak we are afraid our words will not be heard or welcomed. But when we are silent, we are still afraid. So it is better to speak." Spend some time reflecting on this quote, perhaps even journaling about the feelings or ideas it sparks in you. Where are you afraid to speak? How can you begin to overcome that fear?

Chapter 5

Trust Your Mind and Spirit

"I don't know."

Most of us feel very uncomfortable saying those words. We don't want to admit we don't know something, even if we actually don't!

As a parent, I get frustrated when my kids respond to a question with, "I don't know." It's an easy way to avoid explaining their behavior. They often use it when I ask a question that begins, "Why did you..." or "What made you think that was a good idea?"

But I'm realizing "I don't know" is the right answer when we follow it with, "but I'm going to try to learn more and figure it out." In other words, to trust our mind to be able to solve a problem we don't yet know the answer to.

Especially in America, I've noticed we want answers, facts, decisions. And we want those facts to lead to action. But sometimes, what we assume are the facts are not the whole picture. The truth is, sometimes we don't know everything about a given topic. We have more to learn about a situation.

What if, instead of "I don't know," we could say, "Let me put some thought into this." When we admit we need more information and get curious about finding it, we empower ourselves to move forward. We begin to trust our mind and intuition to problem solve. When we move from not knowing to knowing, we build confidence.

Becoming Curious

An essential part of learning self-trust is learning to be curious, to have what is often called "a beginner's mind." Curiosity allows us to not only further our knowledge but also connect with others. Curiosity is a state of mind that demonstrates an interest in collecting the pieces of the puzzle and beginning to assemble a big picture. If we pretend we're already an expert, we miss the opportunity to grow and learn from others.

Being curious leads us to connect with people with whom we don't think we have a lot in common. Curiosity gives us the courage to lean in, to experience new things that we have not tried before. Being curious replaces the fear of failing. My friend Adair, a commercial real estate professional, first introduced me to the phrase "Be curious, not furious."

Apple founder Steve Jobs once said, "You can't connect the dots looking forward, you can only connect dots looking backward. You have to trust that somehow the dots will connect in your future."

I think this is especially true when we think about trying to find meaning, to discover what it means to have faith, and to discover our purpose. By definition it means trusting what will happen, that the dots will connect.

Life is about gaining experience that leads us to our one thing—our calling or purpose. But as you move forward to find your one thing, your purpose, there will be a lot of "dots" along the way until one day, you see them all connecting to where you are.

After two years at Accenture, I was looking for something new, so I decided to take a "career test." At the time, it seemed like a good idea. Looking back, I think that career tests are not very helpful because they point you toward jobs of the past rather than the jobs of tomorrow. It is much more helpful to see how our expertise can be applied to new markets or industries that may interest us and to understand the strengths that we can build on.

The career test suggested that I should consider a career in teaching. When I shared this with my colleagues at work, they literally laughed. I still remember one colleague telling me with a huge smile, "You can't possibly be a teacher, Sylvie." So, I felt stuck. I really did not know what I could do other than consulting and project management.

On my drive to work one morning, I heard on the radio about an organization that taught adults immigrants from Haiti to read and write. It made me curious. I wondered if this might be an opportunity to try teaching without changing careers. So, I called them up and asked if I could volunteer. I was interested in meeting the people and testing myself to see if I could teach. They were happy to have volunteers, so off I went.

That experience revealed a gift that I did not know I had: seeing the potential in people and nudging them out of their comfort zone.

The teacher told me to go through a worksheet with a lady. I'm not really a worksheet type of person. And while the lady struggled with the worksheet, by the end of our session, I could tell she was actually a competent reader. So, the next session, I brought a newspaper with me and asked her to read the front page. I still remember her smile and the spontaneous hug she gave me when she realized that she could read. It warmed my heart. I realized, Yeah, maybe I'm not a classroom teacher, but perhaps there is a way I could be involved in educating adults.

That experience is what got me accepted in the Learning Sciences program at Northwestern University because I shared the story at my admissions interview. Being curious and seizing an opportunity marks one dot on your life path that at some point will connect to another dot down the road.

Have you ever had that sort of pivotal moment? A single experience that points you toward a strength you didn't know you had? If not, why not? Do you allow yourself to be curious, to try things that might stretch you? Because you'll find in those experiences a wealth of information about yourself and who you are, what you're meant to do and be. You will also build new relationships.

Being curious is greater than being opportunistic because it is selfless. Being curious is outward facing—being interested in other people, other situations, other ways of doing things. It is about expanding our comfort zone by putting on hold our thoughts and past experience.

How can you cultivate curiosity? Allow yourself the luxury of paying attention to your own interests and the interests of others. Do something simple but stretching. Go to bird talks, hike on glaciers, ask about how to train for a marathon, and accept invitations to events and gatherings where you don't know anyone. When you meet someone, ask them, "What is your primary focus these days?" Ask what brought them to that industry, that town, that cause, that hobby or sport. Help them connect the dots by asking, "Have you considered representing your community in some capacity?"

Being curious is putting on hold your assumptions and what you think that you already know about an experience. It is about asking who, what, where, why, how questions instead of talking about yourself. In the politically divided world we live in today, being curious means listening to people to understand how they describe systems and how government functions and directly impacts our lives. You will notice that there is rarely a need to state your political affiliation when discussing issues that impact your community.

Being curious also means having the courage to learn about what people do at a deeper level. This way of thinking is useful when you approach a new role or situation. Before bringing your experience, try to understand the context—the past, the present, and the future, the players, the influencers. It is about learning, listening, and then leading. Being curious is also a way of connecting with people and finding out how you can be helpful. It's about asking questions instead of talking about yourself.

For example, not long ago at an event, I introduced myself to one of the guests, who shared that he was from Hawaii. At that moment in the conversation, I could have chosen to talk about myself. I could have shared about my last trip to Hawaii, surfing, my dream of running a marathon there, the delicious island coffee, or about my friend who lives on Easy Street in Maui.

But I decided instead to be curious. So, I asked the gentleman, "What is your focus in Hawaii?" He told me that his company sells hurricane insurance. He had analyzed climate data and was able to offer affordable insurance based on location in the islands.

Again, I chose to be curious. I asked him, "How did you get into insurance? And what brought you to Hawaii?" He told me he had been in a family insurance business all his life in Boston. Eventually, he and his wife decided to retire in Hawaii, but once he was there, he saw an opportunity to offer a specialized and affordable insurance product to residents.

It just so happened that at a recent Policy Circle in Chicago, we had discussed the Government Regulations brief. I'd learned that insurance was a highly regulated industry in each state, so I asked him, "How is insurance regulated specifically in Hawaii?" We talked about how insurance regulations vary from state to state, the role of the federal government, and so on.

I was then able to tell him and his wife about The Policy Circle and how an intentional discussion of government regulations can inform citizens on the burden that regulations can cause to businesses. Entrepreneurs and small businesses are often subject to four levels of regulation: federal, state, county, and municipal. These include licenses, permits, and certificates. These regulations can overlap and conflict, which makes compliance confusing and costly, and sometimes a real barrier for new small innovative enterprises.

We talked about how understanding regulations can spark an interest in streamlining, revaluation, and building in processes that sunset regulations instead of just accepting them.

I remember hearing Horst Schulze, former CEO of Ritz Carlton, speak at the Global Leadership Summit at Willow Creek. He talked about a new hotel that had continuous complaints about room service taking too long. The delivery of food to the rooms was incredibly slow. Schulze talked to the manager in charge of room service, stressing that he needed to step up his game and get people their food.

He also asked his kitchen staff to analyze the process of room service orders. What steps happened from the moment they got a phone call ordering food until the moment they knocked on that person's door with a tray of hot food? The order taking and preparation were highly efficient, but the process snagged when the waiters went to the elevators. Waiters often took as long as 20 minutes to get from the kitchen to the room. Was the problem faulty elevators? Not exactly.

At this point, Schulze could have decreed that the solution was for the waiters to work faster. Or he could have tried to "fix" the elevators to go faster. But instead, Schulze got curious. What did he not know?

As he asked questions, he realized that the problem was not with the kitchen staff, or even the elevators themselves, but rather, with housekeeping. But even they were not ultimately to blame.

The elevators the waiters used were the same ones the houseman used, to transport large carts full of bed linens to the maids. A houseman would frequently block the elevator door with his linen cart in an attempt to get the linens where they needed to go in a timely fashion. But this meant the elevators were stalled wherever the houseman was. That meant he was keeping the waiters, well, waiting.

Eventually, Schulze said, the staff explained that the hotel had only two sets of sheets per bed—one on the bed, the other being laundered. That system created a shortage because the sheets were not ready to be put on a bed when it was changed. The housekeeping staff regularly grabbed sheets from another floor in order to get beds made. And to do that, they parked the laundry cart in the open door of the elevator, in effect hijacking it.

There was another question Schulze didn't know the answer to. Why did this luxury hotel have only two sheet sets per bed? He was told that when the hotel opened, "management" had decreed that in order to save money, they'd only have two instead of three sets of sheets per bed. Naturally, Schulze realized that by his saying "management," the team was politely pointing the finger at him. He'd made that decision, thinking it would save money. Unfortunately, it cost time and customer satisfaction.

It was only when he was willing to become curious, to ask the right questions and hear the sometimes difficult answers, that he was able to correct the problem and solve the issue. Instead of questioning the competence of the people involved, he was curious about the process.

When you start asking why-and-how questions, when you take genuine interest in something that you don't know about, when you are curious, you find solutions. You build connections, you connect dots, you advance, and you enrich your life and that of others.

Beginner's Mind

As you move forward in confidence and develop the ability to trust yourself, you might believe that you should pretend to be an expert, acting as if you know more than you do. And some people do that, telling themselves to "fake it until you make it."

To build trust in yourself, resolve to look at every situation with a "beginner's mind." One of the most intriguing and counterintuitive concepts from Zen Buddhism, the "beginner's mind" approaches every moment, every task, not as an expert but a learner—as if encountering it for the first time. A beginner's mind is full of curiosity—open and ready to learn. When you don't consider anything routine, but, rather, deem each experience new, you live more joyfully. You see possibilities that your "expertise" and "we've always done it this way" mind will miss. When you don't consider yourself an expert, but rather a beginner, you will always be learning and finding creative and innovative ways to approach every situation.

Other faith traditions also teach similar values. The Bible and the Torah both include numerous instructions to be humble, teachings Jesus reinforced when he said that we should approach faith humbly, like a child (see Matthew 18:2-4). It is when we humbly admit we don't know everything that we begin to truly learn. Almost all faith traditions value humility, which is an essential part of a beginner's mind.

When you have a beginner's mind, you can often find creative ways to solve problems. For example, as The Policy Circle grew, I realized it would be helpful to have an audio version of the brief. Some members told me that they used Siri to read the brief to them on their drive home! But I wasn't sure how to create that audio version. I approached the problem with a beginner's mind. I assumed nothing and instead stayed open to learning and finding a creative solution.

At the same time, I found myself invited to be a guest on several podcasts. I enjoyed the experience, knowing that people were listening in. I also enjoy listening to podcasts. So, I thought, Why not use a podcast as a means of creating audio briefs? I'd never done one before, so I was a beginner. As I talked with the team that helps create the written briefs we share, we thought it would be more interesting if we invited an expert to discuss the brief as we read it.

I decided the podcast would be a platform to engage someone who has expertise on the topic and can offer their unique perspective to educate others. But launching a podcast took a bit of courage. I was uncertain. As I started to do research, I knew I had to have a beginner's mind, to admit I didn't know or wasn't an expert.

I love systems, and as I did research on what's involved in putting out a podcast, I realized I could easily get lost in the mechanical details. So when I happened to participate in another podcast and met the producer, I asked if he could partner with us to help us produce a podcast for The Policy Circle. Having a beginner's mind sometimes means you have to partner with someone who has expertise, who can be a guide.

Then, I took a plunge, and we launched the Trust Your Voice podcast. You have to just do it so that you are able to evolve, to learn, and to get feedback from others. You have to be courageous. When you start with a beginner's mind, you can be open and learn. And in a way, the pressure is off. Because you view yourself as a beginner, you can give yourself room to make mistakes and learn from them, rather than expecting perfection right away. Eventually, at least for me, it helped me to sort out what I needed to have others help me with and where I could confidently lead.

I realized that I enjoyed the conversations so much. When you're doing a podcast, you have no choice but to be completely focused. I love that—being fully in the moment and focused on one topic, one person, one task. Doing so gave me renewed energy. It gave me a new perspective on the work we do at The Policy Circle, and it made me proud of the quality of the briefs we produced.

So now, we have a podcast, and in each episode, we read through one of the briefs, but we pause at key points and have a conversation with an expert guest. (You can listen to Trust Your Voice and access the archive at www.sylvielegere.com.)

In developing The Policy Circle framework, my co-founders and I had to adopt a beginner's mind and acknowledge that everyone is different. To engage women, we could not assume that all women were like us. We needed to understand and remove the hurdles that would stop women from starting and leading a circle.

First, we realized they did not want to do it alone, so we decided that circles had to be started by two or three women. Second, we learned that our library of briefs overwhelmed members with too much choice. So, we organized the briefs into groupings of five conversations. Third, we became aware that leaders needed guidance on who to invite. As I explained earlier, we created a system to make it simple and yet get a variety of people: Each of the three women invites one person, to make up six participants. Each of those six each invites one person, which brings the total to 12 people. We also suggest a variety in geography, in experience/profession, and in diversity to have all voices enrich the conversation. The only criterion is people who want to learn, listen, and engage constructively. But fine-tuning the process of the onboarding came only when we listened with an open mind to others and acknowledged that people process experiences differently.

Adopting a beginner's mind in small things, even in your daily routine, cultivates the habit. It's called a practice for a reason—you have to practice this attitude and openness in small things if you ever hope to have it in critical situations. Because it is hard, you have to be humble and intentional.

If you make it your practice to see life in this way, you will, indeed, grow in wisdom and experience. Continually cultivating an attitude of open curiosity and compassion will allow that growth to continue. This attitude, which the Japanese call *shoshin,* will not only contribute to your own satisfaction and peace, it will transform your relationships with others.

Confidence grows not just from saying "I think I can" but from actually doing and accomplishing. You have to jump in and try things and allow yourself to make mistakes. But along with making mistakes, you'll do many things right. Then you can apply your past experience to new situations. When you achieve even something minor, your confidence and trust in yourself grows. A beginner's mind will lead you to achievement because it opens your mind to innovation. You'll also build your confidence because you will grow in competence, which should impact your career in a positive way.

In her article "How to Cultivate a Beginner's Mind to Become a True Expert," coach Marta Brzosko writes:

"Maintaining an open mind of a beginner is essential if you are trying to innovate, but also if you want to become an expert in any field. This is because moving to the next level of skill or knowledge often demands letting go of beliefs and attitudes acquired at earlier stages of learning. In other words, mastering any skill or field of expertise requires you to constantly revise what you assume you already know."[23]

Even if you are mentoring someone else, approach your interactions with a beginner's mind. What is this person feeling? What challenges are they facing? What can you learn from them, even though you are their mentor? How can you learn to be a better mentor even as you interact with your mentee?

If you are being mentored, this stance is easier—as the point of mentoring is to seek out the wisdom and advice of a more experienced person. A beginner's mind keeps you from being defensive when they offer you corrections or advice. It allows you to approach each meeting or interaction with your mentor as a fresh, new experience.

It may seem counterintuitive, but a beginner's mind will help you to build self-trust. You trust that each day you can learn new things and grow. You trust that the pressure's off. You don't have to be an expert or have all the answers, you simply need to be open, curious, and eager to learn and experience new things.

In his book *Zen Mind, Beginner's Mind*, Shunryu Suzuki writes: "The beginner's mind is the mind of compassion. When our mind is compassionate, it is boundless."[24] Sometimes the hardest person to have compassion for is yourself. That is why self-trust is foundational to other trusts. And if you have compassion for yourself, you will come to trust yourself, your voice, your convictions.

Releasing Our Potential

Being comfortable with not knowing releases potential within us. When we embrace the beginner's mind, the learner's posture, we find we have the

---

23 From an article by Marta Brzosko found at: https://betterhumans.coach.me/how-to-cultivate-beginners-mind-to-become-a-true-expert-b2e82953318d

24 See *Zen Mind, Beginner's Mind* at http://amzn.to/2ftRrsV

infinite potential to grow. To remain open and curious, we must admit that there are things we don't know and be thankful we have the opportunity to learn. Would you rather be a know-it-all or a lifelong learner? And paradoxically, admitting we don't have it all figured out actually helps us to trust ourselves more fully.

One of the goals of The Policy Circle is to allow members to learn to be okay with not knowing, and also to open them up to the fact that they can be learners, that they can increase their expertise and understanding on a topic. They can form an opinion, not just based on what other people or the news media tells them, but on their own understanding.

How do they gain that understanding? As our culture relies increasingly on social media and sound bites, people are losing their ability to critically think through various issues. They seem almost unable to grasp nuance, instead wanting everything oversimplified terms. The way to gain understanding is to trust your mind, which comes from spending time thinking, reading, asking questions, and being curious. Sometimes, issues are complicated. We should be willing to explore and study the big picture before forming an opinion.

One of our frustrations when we first started with The Policy Circle was that some of the members of a circle would come to the meetings without reading the brief. It was as if they didn't trust themselves to understand and interpret it. They seemed to lack the confidence to simply sit and read and try to understand. People didn't trust themselves to read and step out of their comfort zone.

If they didn't read the brief, there was less risk. They didn't have to step out, offer an opinion, and risk people possibly disagreeing with them. They didn't have to defend a position. It was easier, in some ways, to not have any opinion at all. They didn't trust their mind, so they didn't use their voice.

So, part of what we do is teach members how to trust their mind enough to ask good questions. We're providing a safe place to learn. We want them to become comfortable with not knowing everything, but also with trusting their mind enough to move past "I don't know" to a place where they can ask insightful questions that will help them grow intellectually. And while we want them to learn and understand the issues, that is not the sole purpose of The Policy Circle. We also have a vision for helping members make connections—networking. We want women who have more experience to help those who are younger or not as far along in their career.

When you read and comprehend and trust your mind enough to say what you think, then you will connect with others. They may agree with you, or even disagree with you, but you can engage in a dialogue about the issue at hand. With expanded knowledge and ability to ask questions, you will quickly find commonality with people. And that allows you to connect and then network.

I hope that The Policy Circle will help members trust their mind enough to know which issues matter most to them. And then, to connect with others who also have a passion or concern that aligns with theirs. And finally, to turn that concern into action.

Trusting your mind gives you the confidence to go out into other contexts—business, politics, community involvement, whatever. The Policy Circle is a place where women can practice trusting their mind, using their voice. And they can make connections, build meaningful friendships, and look for new career opportunities.

A Wild Goose

I grew up without much connection to spiritual things. For years, I considered myself agnostic or atheist. But that is slowly changing. I am becoming more aware that each of us has within us a spirit, or a soul, an essential part of us that is not just our mind, but something deeper than our rationality.

And trusting your voice means also trusting your spirit.

As I've continued to explore spirituality, I wondered about the Holy Spirit. I'd always pictured Him as a hovering dove, a rather passive, vague, peaceful sort of presence. Peaceful, but sort of boring, honestly. But then I learned that the ancient Celtic people's name for the Holy Spirit was "Ah Geadh-Glas," the wild goose. I first heard about this from Sally Blount, former dean of the Kellogg School of Management at Northwestern University. Considering that meaning changed a lot for me.

I imagined that the Holy Spirit or grace would bring peace, and we're always seeking inner peace, tranquility. That's what I thought the goal was. That deep contemplative mode is not something that comes naturally to me. But I thought, Okay, if I'm going to connect with my spirit, I need to connect with the dove, the calm, the quiet. I need to do meditation to find inner peace, find calm, find Zen.

But then I heard Sally speak about this idea of a wild goose. She said, "Inner peace is not the goal of life. The goal is compassion and an open heart to suffering in the world around us." She asked, "What if the Holy Spirit is not a dove but a wild white goose?" This image of the wild goose is quite thought provoking to me. It shifts the paradigm. Now the goal is not inner peace. Instead, it's movement. It's purpose. What a revelation. I'm much more fascinated by a wild white goose than a dove.

Similarly, Philip Kosloski writes: "The ancient Celtic people saw the Holy Spirit not as a hovering white dove but as a 'wild goose.' The meaning behind this peculiar choice is because they saw how the Holy Spirit has a tendency to disrupt and surprise. The Holy Spirit moves in our lives in an unexpected fashion, similar to the actions of a wild goose."[25]

In his book *Wild Goose Chase*, which explores this idea, Mark Batterson writes: "I understand that 'wild goose chase' typically refers to a purpose-less endeavor without a defined destination. But chasing the Wild Goose is different. The promptings of the Holy Spirit can sometimes *seem* pretty pointless, but rest assured, God is working His plan. And if you chase the Wild Goose, He will take you places you never could have imagined going by paths you never knew existed."[26]

I enjoy solitude when I want to recharge. There are times for contemplation, for rest, for silent retreat. But there is an inner resolve and a sense of joy that comes when you can simply let yourself follow the wild goose instead of feeling like you have to work really hard to just be quiet. (Working hard to be still is sort of an oxymoron anyway, isn't it?)

So, following the Spirit is not only about stillness and waiting, but movement and purpose. I began to see that things happening in my life that seem like chasing a wild goose were happening for a reason, for a purpose. This idea of disruption and surprise is disconcerting, but it's been exactly

---

25 How the wild goose became a symbol of vigilance and the Holy Spirit"
by Phlip Kosloski, Oct. 2, 2017, found at https://aleteia.org/2017/10/02/
how-the-wild-goose-became-a-symbol-of-vigilance-and-the-holy-spirit/
26 Batterson, Mark. *Wild Goose Chase*. Grand Rapids, MI: Zondervan. 2008, 2.

my experience. And rather than try to avoid it, I'm learning it's okay to just follow the wild white goose. A "wild goose chase" is actually a spiritual journey. Thinking of the spirit as a wild goose helped me to move forward in trusting my own spirituality because it fit better with who I am.

I've become more curious about faith of all kinds and how it impacts people.

My cousin, Kirstin, and I had a number of conversations about faith. Through these conversations, she was inspired to start a blog to write about her Christian faith and how it guides her life. (The blog is at https://www. holdlooselylivefreely.com/)

So, part of my spiritual journey is reading Scripture, reading blogs like Kirstin's, and just being open-minded to talk about faith.

My kids attended a Catholic school, and faith has become an important part of their lives, and I'm really glad about that.

As I get more comfortable with trusting my own spirit, I find that I have more hope. I'm realizing my past struggles with depression and hopelessness had to do with not having faith that I am part of a bigger plan. So, I'm on a journey, still trying to learn and understand, and to embrace gratitude, love, forgiveness and grace.

Learning to trust your voice means you must also trust your mind and your spirit. The inner you, which is longing to express itself, must be cultivated and encouraged.

You're Invited

Often, we don't trust our mind and our soul because we somehow feel we're not invited. Men and women alike often suffer from an "imposter syndrome" where they lack confidence. They mistakenly believe someone will figure out that they really don't know what they are talking about. The Policy Circle combats that with actual experience. You read the brief, and you share your thoughts—you don't have to be an expert, you just have to prepare, show up, and speak up. Doing that builds confidence; it helps us trust our voice. And Policy Circles all over the country are giving women a platform to do just that.

For example, several of the women from an Indianapolis circle, including Katie Glick, Clare Morrison, Morgan Perrill, and Lacey Willard, had the opportunity to lead a plenary session at the Indianapolis Chamber of Commerce's sixth annual Women in Business Retreat. The theme was "impact," and the retreat was billed as a way for women from all professional backgrounds to escape their hectic life and learn from one another, share successes, laugh, network, and strategize about what comes next.

These women taught a session titled "Your License to Influence." They gave an overview of The Policy Circle's approach and a primer on a poverty mini-brief specific to Indiana. They then hosted a circle discussion with the nearly 200 attendees, followed by recaps and Q&A, just as we do at The Policy Circle meetings. They were able to share our vision and offered a simple strategy: "Learn the Facts. Discuss the Issues. Start the Conversation."

The Policy Circle women said they found the attendees ready for real conversation, influence, and impact. They were gratified to notice that throughout the rest of the two-day retreat, many presenters referenced their session while on stage, several attendees sought information on starting circles, and they received feedback that theirs was one of the most engaging sessions of the retreat.

I loved hearing about this, because these women took the platform to the next level. Here are just a few things local Circles or their members have done to invite others into the conversation and make an impact:

- In Michigan, one of the Pioneer Cohort Circles is called Friends of Pam. It started in July 2017. There are 22 women in this circle. Three members ran for office in 2018 with one, Andrea Schroder, winning a state representative seat. Their circle leader, Deb O'Hagan, has gone on to mentor the beginning of another circle in Michigan.
- In Wisconsin, the El Circulo group is a Circle of Hispanic women who have chosen to mentor young Hispanic girls by hosting Policy Circle meetings geared toward them. They see how important it is for this information to be taught at a young age. Tammy, the circle leader, is involved in fundraising for a local private school and is a leader in her community.

- In Colorado, Erica Shields, circle leader, has become very involved in fighting against what she sees as government overreach in the schools. She has gone to the state capitol to speak to this and other issues that she feels strongly about. She is a professional public-health educator specializing in research. She's also a mom who just pulled her child out to homeschool because of her concerns about the direction of Colorado schools. She is trying to get appointed to a local board.
- Dee Dee Bass Wilbon and Deana Bass Williams (#TheBassSisters) are part of a Policy Circle in Maryland. They decided to start a podcast called "Policy and Pound Cake," where they share weekly wisdom on politics and culture.[27]
- Patricia Kempthorne, member of a Policy Circle in Boise, Idaho, started the Twiga Foundation in 2005. Twiga means Giraffe in Swahili. Twiga is dedicated to inspiring, promoting, and maintaining a family consciousness at home, in the workplace, and in the community. The Twiga Foundation is the fiscal sponsor for the Parenting in the Workplace Institute (PIWI), allowing each organization to fulfill their mission for family consciousness in the workplace. PIWI researches and provides resources for the implementation of formal programs in which parents can bring their children to work every day and care for them while doing their jobs.[28]

These women are speaking up and getting involved in their communities, in politics, in local schools. They are discovering that they can make a difference and connect with others to do that. They are learning that their voice and words have impact, and they matter.

We spend a lot of time trying to get others to do things, trying to influence others. If we put as much effort into developing ourselves as we put into trying to change others, we'd see real change.

What is Your Lens?
We expect participants to read the brief before they attend The Policy Circle meetings. Then we go around the circle, and each person gets to speak. We

27 Listen or subscribe at https://www.buzzsprout.com/1024030
28 Learn more at http://www.twigafoundation.org/projects.html

give them a two-minute hourglass timer so they have to be concise, and no one can dominate.

The question we ask is simple, but it invites people to share without becoming argumentative: What is the lens through which you read this brief?

We all observe the world through lenses, through our experiences and the information we've gathered in the past. We sort through new information in our mind, using the filters and information we already have stored there. It profoundly colors the way we see anything.

That's why two people can read the same policy brief, the same information, but see the issues very differently. This has to do not only with the sphere of care and horizon of care we discussed previously, but the life experiences that have shaped them. So, when we ask them not just what they think of the brief and the issues presented in it, but also about the lens through which they view it, it forces them to think about their thinking. This meta-thinking allows them to step back, to notice their own bias or point of view. In a way, it helps them to understand their own thinking more clearly—which is the first step to trusting your mind.

We try to avoid political labels like Republican or Democrat, liberal or conservative. Rather, we ask, what do you think of the ideas, and what lens do you view them through? Sometimes people assume they should wear a certain label, but when they actually think through the issue, their opinions align with a different label, a different ideology.

Sharing about your lens, or your focus, is really sharing about your life. Are you an entrepreneur, or are you climbing the corporate ladder? Is your main focus your career, your family—or perhaps, are you struggling to balance them both? Are you a highly spiritual person who looks through a lens of faith or religion? Or is something else a priority? What problem are you trying to solve with the work you do?

An unexpected benefit of The Policy Circle is that it helps members to become more self-aware. They share ideas and realize not everyone thinks the same thing they do or sees the world in the same way. They sort through issues to figure out what they actually think. That's sometimes a problem in our culture—people don't know what they really think, so they just respond in the moment. We invite members to think it through, to really consider all sides of an issue and the implications of taking a position.

There's an old saying, "Only fools don't change their mind." When we gain insights by discussing and studying issues, we might change our mind. We might grow into a more nuanced position. If you trust your mind, you're comfortable with changing it as you learn and grow. Your mind can expand, explore, and connect with others in new ways.

Many of us grew up with these messages: Don't be needy, be self-sufficient, and don't let others see your weakness. When we surrender to the truth, it doesn't mean we give up. It doesn't mean we hide in a hole and complain, but rather, we develop our own strategies to move forward. We find ways to be willing to ask for help from others.

Ironically, an essential component of building self-trust is realizing you can't do it all and reaching out to the people around you to ask for help. And that's what we will turn to in the next chapter.

Trust Challenge:

What do you think it means to have a "beginner's mind"? What is one situation you're currently facing where you could try this approach?

What is your response to the idea of thinking of God or the Holy Spirit as a "wild goose"? How does that idea compare to the traditions you grew up with or are now a part of?

Think about the role, if any, that faith and spirituality play in your life. Draw a circle that represents your life's priorities. Where does faith fit in? Is it a tiny slice? The center? All pervasive? Nonexistent? Without judgment, reflect on where you are now. Allow yourself to become curious about where you would like to be.

Chapter 6

Trust That You Can Build a Strong Network

Women have more opportunities today than they've ever had. And we work very hard. What holds us back as women is not a lack of knowledge, a shortage of skills, or not having the desire to succeed.

The thing that sometimes keeps us from reaching our full potential (I include myself in this) is that we don't trust that others want to connect with us, to help us. A study published in the journal *Human Relations* suggests that men and women build their networks differently. Women are hesitant to network, to rely on the help that others would be willing to give us. Or we attempt to connect but are hesitant to ask others for the help we need. We're not even sure what to ask for. We're conditioned to be givers, but networking is about both give and take.

When women seek a mentor, the study says, they tend to look for someone they want to be friends with rather than someone they can learn from. Studies have shown women aren't getting the tough feedback they need to move ahead. The best mentors will push, dare, and confront mentees, and challenge them to take on projects they might otherwise avoid.

Men, on the hand, look to form alliances. Men are willing to do business with anyone, even someone they don't necessarily like, as long as that person can help them achieve their goals. Men understand that this is a work relationship that can be dissolved when it's no longer convenient, not a long-term friendship. Yet women are leery of capitalizing on social ties and tend to overemphasize the moral aspects of networking, the study finds.[29]

Alexis Krivkovich, a managing partner for McKinsey's Silicon Valley office and an author of the 2018 Women in the Workplace study by McKinsey & Co. and LeanIn.org, recommends that you be deliberate in creating that network by mapping out which person you would ask for career advice, for sponsorship, for a sounding board, and to challenge you. "Understand what role you are hoping for—sponsorship, mentorship, or an ally," Krivkoich writes. "Sponsorship is about opportunity creation, mentorship is about advice, and an ally equates to someone who will be your personal champion. There are a range of roles you want to have in a network to make it robust."[30]

Ironically, in order to trust yourself, you have to trust others. You have to believe that other people want to connect with you.

Think about a time you helped someone. It feels good to help, to see someone seize an opportunity that you perhaps guided them toward. People want to feel helpful. Do you trust that others would get that same satisfaction from helping you? Do others want to help and guide you? It goes back to human nature—that you matter, and others matter too. People want to know that they matter to you, and when you help them, you feel good about yourself. And you can trust that they'll return the favor.

In The Policy Circle people discover and trust that others want to connect with them. It also provides them opportunities in their career. They come together to discuss policy, through that discussion they share experience, priorities, goals and challenges at work, at home, in the community. The Policy Circle provides a forum to establish a connection, expand and diversify a network, find allies, and mentors. The women in The Policy

29 See https://journals.sagepub.com/doi/10.1177/0018726718804303
and The hidden gap between men and women networking by Lisa Rabasca
Roepe for Fast Company: https://www.fastcompany.com/90277129/
the-hidden-networking-gap-between-men-and-women
30 See https://www.mckinsey.com/featured-insights/gender-equality/
women-in-the-workplace-2018

Circle benefit, they grow professionally and personally, and then, they turn around and help others. It's exciting to watch. The Policy Circle is a platform to build an inner circle and also expand our network by inviting men and women to a substantive conversation.

The way to learn to trust that others want to connect with you begins with taking a risk and making a connection. For me, starting The Policy Circle pulled me out of my comfort zone, and I realized I couldn't do it alone. As people came together, I looked around in wonder. Some truly amazing women saw the vision for what The Policy Circle could be, and they wanted to connect with me and with each other. I began to trust them, and we accomplished far more than any of us could have done alone.

You matter. But everybody else wants to know that they matter to you. So, it's important to invest in relationships.

Connecting with others is about validating people, making them feel dignified in whatever it is they do. Servers, cashiers, parking people—everyone matters, and when you treat them that way, they respond. My dad did that really well, he always sought out other people's opinions and never hesitated to engage with people randomly at restaurants, parks, or festivals. He talked to leaders in various industries and communities. He hasn't been mayor for decades, but people still call him The Mayor. I admit, I'm often more task-focused than people-focused, but I try to learn from the way my dad did things and treat people the way he did.

Know Thyself

Personality tests such asthe Enneagram, the DiSC test, StrengthsFinder, Living Languages are incredibly helpful to identify strengths and areas for improvement.

Every time I take a test, I end up with labels like Reformer, Achiever, or Challenger. I don't like to admit it, but I score low on harmony and empathy. I like to get stuff done and to surround myself with strong action oriented people. As an achiever, I feel like I always have to prove my value. And if you're a challenger, you challenge injustice, stick up for the underdog. But you intimidate the very people you are trying to help because you have this strong personality.

Knowing yourself and your strengths (and weaknesses) is an essential step to connecting with others. By knowing yourself, you can see what you have to offer and what you need from others, that's the basis of building a strong broad network.

Filling in the Gaps

When you know where you need help, you can reach out to others to fill in the gaps, and create a powerful team.

Starting The Policy Circle forced me outside of myself. It required me to accurately assess not only my strengths but also to acknowledge the places where I needed help. I had to gather a team of people to fill the gaps in my knowledge and competencies. I was good at some things, but no one is good at all things.

When you start a nonprofit, you quickly realize that to keep the lights on and accomplish your mission, you need donations. Donations come from people and organizations that believe in both the mission and the leadership of the organization. To find that, you need to build relationships with people and create a community of people who want to support the organization, who believe in its mission enough to invest in it.

Fundraising, and the people skills it requires, is not my strength. I knew I needed someone who was an "Influencer" on the DiSC test. While I brought my strength as a process person, someone who can turn an idea into reality, I knew I needed a team that included someone with different strengths, whose skills and aptitudes complemented mine.

Fortunately Kathy Hubbard, my Policy Circle co-founder, is a tremendous connector, influencer and cheerleader. Kathy shared so much experience as founder of Bridges of Understanding, a non-profit, non-political group working to advance understanding between Americans and people in the Arab world. Her energy and wide network fueled the growth of The Policy Circle. She is gregarious; she is all about knowing people, connecting people. She illuminates a room when she walks in. When we work together, we can each lean into our own strengths. I need people like her to push me, to make me realize that I bring value to others, and to remind me that people want to connect with me.

When you know yourself, your blind spots, and the goals that you are trying to achieve, it is easy to ask for and accept help from people who bring diverse sets of strengths. That's how you grow, that's how you build.

Vulnerability

Connecting with others requires vulnerability.

Vulnerability is accepting who we are with our strengths and our weaknesses. In order to be vulnerable, we must know ourselves. We must be willing to open our eyes to who we are and who we are not.

All of us have blind spots—faults we cannot see, often because we have carefully constructed blinders, or even walls, to protect our reputation or self-image. But when we are willing to stop and look at who we are and accept our imperfections, they are no longer blind spots. They are simply who we are. We can seek out mentors and collaborators whose strengths complement our own. In order to do that, we have to admit that we need help, that we can't do everything perfectly! (By the way, everyone else already knows that.)

Vulnerability invites us to stop building an armor around ourselves and instead, become authentic. Vulnerability allows us to stop thinking, "I should…" (what others want me to do) and begin thinking, "In my opinion…" (what I actually believe) and be okay with that. In her book, *Daring Greatly*, Brené Brown describes vulnerability as "uncertainty, risk, and emotional exposure." It's that unstable feeling we get when we step out of our comfort zone or do something that forces us to loosen control. However, she notes, "Vulnerability is the birthplace of love, belonging, joy, courage, empathy, and creativity."[31]

If there is a gap between what you say and what you know and believe, that gap is filled with insecurity, anger and fear. Often, that anger comes from assuming that other people expect us to be perfect. We're angry that they won't accept us when we make mistakes. But the truth is, other people's expectations of us are rarely as high as we assume. There is something about vulnerability and imperfection that invites connection.

---

31 Brown, Brené. *Daring Greatly.* New York: Avery/Penguin Random House LLC. 2012. 34.

So, vulnerability is about saying what you think and thinking about what you say. It's about walking the talk, knowing what you are good at and what you are not so good at and accepting it. When you do that, you can accept others with their weaknesses as well. And that opens the door to collaboration. Their strengths differ from yours, and together you can accomplish far more than anyone could working alone.

Trust Challenge:

 Do you have people who can be part of your personal board of advisors? If not, list three individuals who you turn to for advice or wish you had turned to. What is your next step in assembling your personal board of advisors? How can you broaden your network in other industries, other professions, other cultures? How can you expand your network vertically towards your leadership goals by finding commonality? Have you considered expanding your network to political circles with locally elected officials?

Starting a Policy Circle may give you a platform to expand your ecosystem of relationships.

In this and other chapters, we've discussed personality tests. Look online to find an assessment for DiSC, Life Languages, StrengthsFinder, or other personality tests. Take at least one of these tests and discuss what you've discovered about yourself with a friend, or consider getting a coach.

Chapter 7

Trust in the Process, Even if It Takes a While

The Policy Circle provides a place to increase civic knowledge and grow in confidence to trust your voice. By engaging in a process of reading, thinking, and sharing our ideas, we are transformed. Our confidence often turns into action.

For some, the goal is simply to be more informed, understand how local and national government works, and engage their minds and hearts in meaningful discussion. Those are great goals, and that process is exhilarating and rewarding. Others want to engage more fully, to find a way to not just understand, but influence.

As we saw hunger to lead and make change, we decided to create a curriculum that was process-based, to take participants from having general civic knowledge to becoming civic leaders. We called upon Kim Borchers who had experience at every level of government and activism. She is a dynamo who started her activism by fighting against pornography at her local public library, and became chief of staff for Governor Sam Brownback in Kansas. Kim codified her experience and created The Policy Circle's Civic Leader Engagement Roadmap, or CLER.

CLER works with emerging leaders to grow their impact through civic engagement. This innovative, action-oriented curriculum was designed to educate, prepare, and build the next generation of public leaders. The curriculum facilitates an understanding of the American founding principles that live on today and features one-on-one coaching, mastermind peer groups, networking opportunities, and specific activities designed to build local connections with policy leaders and decision-makers.

The program is very hands-on, and experiential. Participants learn and study, but also must engage and take action. In order to "graduate" from CLER, each participant must:

- Attend local government meetings (city council, for example)
- Schedule a meeting with their local council representative
- Discover key leaders who influence elections
- Write, submit, and publish an op-ed article in a local or national publication

"CLER helped me to affirm my values," says Jamee Lock, a graduate of the program. "I appreciated knowing about opposing views as it helped me to be educated about all sides of the issues. Also, as a result of CLER, I did in-depth research of two candidates in the November 2020 elections to really understand what they were running for."

Jamee got involved politically by simply following her interests. "I applied online and was offered an appointment on a Housing Commission because of my prior work history with Habitat for Humanity," she says.

As a result of participating in CLER, Lindsay Hannah told me that she had the courage to start attending city council meetings, and she wrote an op-ed in her local paper. "The depth of material provided through the CLER program strengthened my political knowledge base more than I could have imagined," she says. "As one who desires to run for political office someday, the CLER program builds confidence, knowledge, and connections that will last a lifetime."

These participants have found that if they trust the process, they're able to accomplish and influence far more than they ever imagined. Trusting the process applies not only to political involvement but also to seemingly small and ordinary events. These events and decisions shape our lives for the better if we're willing to engage.

Fact-Based Decision Making

There is always an opportunity to teach project management and fact-based decision-making. The best tool I have taught my kids is the decision matrix. This is a standard tool companies use for selecting a vendor for a project. My daughter first learned to use the decision matrix when deciding which high school to attend. Did she want a public or private school? If private, which one? Choosing a school that fits your child's learning style and personality, and also your family's values, is a truly empowering family experience.

In Quebec, students can choose which high school they want to go to because each school has a different focus. Some might specialize in science and math, while others provide vocational training for the trades, and so on. Learning styles, abilities, interests are different for everyone. Families should have a choice in schools beyond their zip code based on school performance and teaching approaches. In a country that celebrates individual accomplishments, choice, and excellence, choice in education should be available to everyone. This would bring innovation, specialization, and competition, as it did in Quebec. In Quebec, private schools receive subsidies and a portion of private school tuition is tax deductible[32], and families can request to enroll in schools outside their geographic boundaries.

Even within the system here, I wanted my kids to make the decision about their school themselves.

To make it a thoughtful process, we developed a decision matrix identifying the criteria that were important to them and assigning a weight to each criterion. For example, a decision matrix might include criteria like location, clubs, academic rigor, social life, potential scholarships, sense of community, technology, faith etc. Then, after each visit, they assigned a rating to each criterion. The sum of the weight multiplied by the rating adds up to a score that can be used to rationally compare each school. The

---

32 Details on the Canadian tax code as it relates to school fees can be found at https://www.taxtips.ca/filing/privateschool.htm

tool removes the emotion and takes us beyond the "I like it vs. I don't like it." The process gives confidence in the final decision.

Process can build confidence and trust. But process requires pen to paper, and it takes longer. As a result of using the decision matrix, my children each decided to attend a Catholic school. I felt the process was really empowering for each of my kids, at a young age, to own that decision. Going through this exercise made them really confident about their choice. But it also gave them a tool that they can use in other decisions. My daughter now uses the decision matrix in almost every big decision she has to make. It's a tool that becomes part of the decision making process and gives you confidence in your decision.

Inviting Others into the Process
As I mentioned in the last chapter, when my husband and his friend purchased the local bike shop and were trying to turn it around, I jumped into bicycling and tried to inspire other women to ride bikes too. I hosted group rides, organized clinics, and encouraged women to take time for themselves and to invest in a good bike. It was a fun way to build our business and foster community and connection for women.

But I'm really more of a runner than a biker. When I moved to Chicago I joined a running group—The Chicago Area Runners Association (CARA). They sponsor training runs and races, and they provided a great way to meet people who shared my interest in fitness. Through CARA, I heard about a gentleman who planned to run 50 miles for his 50th birthday. He asked people to join him to run part of his 50-mile run. I didn't really know him, but several of us decided it would be fun to be part of this epic celebration.

I was only in my early 30s when I ran a segment of that 50-mile run. It inspired me. I thought, someday, I want to try something like that. So, the year I was turning 40, I decided to set a big goal for myself—to run 40 miles on my 40th birthday. By that point, I had run several marathons. I knew what it meant to trust the training process, slowly building up my endurance with longer and longer runs. But a marathon is 26.2 miles, and 40 miles is, well, a lot!

Any goal requires a process to complete it. A 40-mile run meant training for almost a year. It also meant planning a route to run on the actual day since I wasn't competing in a race or event. Friends wanted to be part of the experience, so I set up a course around our town. This allowed various people to join me for segments of the run. My goal had been perhaps to prove that age wasn't going to slow me down, but the run had an unexpected benefit. As I trained, and on the day I actually ran, I noticed how excited people were to be a part of what I was doing. I ended up building a community without expecting that to happen.

I was touched, and am even to this day, in a way that I did not expect. About 40 people joined me, running segments from five miles to 10 miles of my run. I had set up three loops of 10 miles and then two loops of five miles, each loop starting and ending in a local park, where there were bagels and coffee. We started at five in the morning and ended at one in the afternoon. The day ended with a party.

When you trust the process, good things happen. When you invite others into the process, you can achieve more than you thought possible. People have the chance to see what you are doing and join in.

Trusting the process means developing patience with yourself and with others. It's realizing that certain things take time, but that time is not wasted. It's not idle waiting, but a type of building, during which you grow stronger, more confident, more capable. You may want things to happen quickly, but when they happen over time (like training to run 40 miles), people have time to catch the vision and get inspired by your goals.

Trusting the process also helps you to get clarity about what you're doing, where you're going, and who is coming with you. Inviting others to be part of the process is the greatest way to connect with people.

Clear Process Means High Quality
Early in my career, I was introduced to quality management practices. Quality standards, such as ISO 9000 and ISO 9001, help companies qualitatively measure their work. One key concept in quality management is the idea of a process-based approach. Essentially, a process-based approach analyzes key tasks by breaking them down into input, process, and output.

A process-based approach means understanding every step of a process so that we can make sure things are being done correctly. When the process is clear and spelled out, quality improves. It all starts with clear and measurable outcomes. From there, the steps to get to the outcome can be broken down at the simplest level. The steps can be repeated and the flywheel starts.

We can break down the process and we can change things that are not helping us move efficiently from input to the desired output.

A few years ago, I heard Melinda Gates speak. Like me, Melinda studied computer science in the early 1990s. In her talk, she pointed out that women today make up a low percentage of the workforce in technology. Indeed, according to Adeva IT,[33] as of 2018, women held only 25 percent of all the jobs in the tech industry, despite women making up almost half of the total workforce. What's worse, this number is lower than the percentage of tech jobs held by women back in the 1980s. It is the only field where the participation of women went down.[34]

According to the *Wall Street Journal*, "Over the past two decades, the number of bachelor's degrees China awards annually has more than quadrupled and now exceeds that of America, the European Union, and Japan combined. Two decades ago, American researchers published four times more peer-reviewed articles in the science and engineering disciplines than their counterparts in China. China received fewer than 20,000 patents two decades ago, but this figure rose to more than 400,000 by 2018, exceeding annual U.S. patent grants by more than 100,000."[35]

Over the last several decades, opportunities within science, technology, engineering, and mathematics (commonly referred to as STEM subjects) have increased for women. The problem is, women and girls do not take advantage of those opportunities. According to a 2017 Women In Tech report by Pricewaterhouse Coopers,[36] among the students participating in the research, more boys opted for STEM subjects compared to girls, except for biology. This is true both in high school and in university.

---

33 See https://adevait.com/state-of-women-in-tech%22%20%5Ct%20%22_blank

34 See https://www.isemag.com/2020/10/telecom-the-latest-stats-on-women-in-tech/

35 See https://www.wsj.com/articles/
stepping-up-the-tech-fight-against-china-11614709490

36 https://www.pwc.co.uk/who-we-are/women-in-technology.html

The report also found:

- About 83 percent of boys in high school opt for STEM subjects, while only 64 percent of girls opt for STEM subjects.
- In high school, 17 percent of boys study physics, compared to just 7 percent of girls.
- The same gender disparity is evident at the university, where 52 percent of males take STEM-related courses, in contrast to only 30 percent of females.
- The gap is even bigger when it comes to courses like engineering. About 13 percent of the surveyed male university students were taking engineering courses, compared to just 2 percent of female university students.
- Despite the recent progress, women head up only about 8 percent of all Fortune 500 companies.

So, these are the facts. I have three children, and I decided that I would do whatever I could to encourage them to pursue studies in STEM. High schoolers need to imagine themselves in the C-suite. They need to imagine themselves pursuing studies and careers in STEM. They need role models so that they know what is possible. So, I initiated a program at my daughter's all-girl high school called "Imagine Yourself in the C-Suite," where women in leadership roles in technology, science, and finance would come to the school and present their journey to the students. The goal is to inspire the students to take that journey to study science or finance and aspire to the highest levels of leadership.

When launching this type of initiative, it is critical to have allies in the school administration and other parents to ensure that the program lives on. Another challenge is to maintain focus and stay true to the mission, and this is where "having a process" becomes important. As we rolled out this program at the school, many parents and friends had suggestions throughout the year to invite lawyers, human resources executives, or marketing executives who would be great speakers. We needed a clear way to stay focused on leaders in STEM.

So, we developed a process to select the speakers. They had to be C-level leaders in science, technology, or finance; we would identify speakers a year in advance; and we would invite three speakers a year. We established key planning milestones throughout the year. When you have criteria and a process, then it is easy to stay focused and engage others constructively.

The other key to a successful process is to have a champion who owns and refines the process. However, wherever there is an issue, instead of turning to the people, think about the process and guardrails you could put in place to ensure, regardless of the people, the objectives will be achieved.

In this case, everyone had ideas about who to invite to speak or topics to talk about. I had to say, "Time out. The goal is to get our youth to move toward careers in STEM. Here are the statistics, and the goal is to change those. We want to move the number in those fields." That helped keep the program focused.

Today, the program is still ongoing at my daughter's former school. Other parents are involved. Other people have ownership. This example can help you when you are applying process-based thinking to more complex situations, such as how you approach your work, meet a personal goal, or advocate for change in society.

On a personal level, you can apply process-based thinking to almost any goal. For example, when someone says they want to be in shape, well, the process is simple, but it begins with an important step—advance decision-making. That is, decide ahead of time what you will do. Don't wait until you "feel like" working out. Don't say, Should I exercise today, or no? (Because you know how that might go.)

Pick a time, the same time every day, and set it aside for working out. It may be five in the morning or six at night, but be consistent. Then, at that time, there is not an option. You work out because it is your workout time. Make it part of your routine, something you have decided ahead of time, not something you have to choose in the moment. Choose your workout routine and clothes the day before so there is no time wasted and commit to it. That's process. And it leads to consistent action, which leads to success.

When a company takes a process-based approach to its work, they "break down each process to understand the following: How is it done? When is it done? Who does it? What is needed to get done? How do you know it is working effectively?"[37]

---

37 From https://factorquality.com/process-approach/#:~:text=What%20is%20 Process%2Dbased%20Approach,process%20feeds%20into%20the%20next.

We've taken this same approach as we've built The Policy Circle.

The Power of the Talking Stick

Have you ever sat in a group meeting where one person dominates the conversation for the duration of the meeting? How do you break in? In her TED talk and book *Quiet: The Power of Introverts in A World That Can't Stop Talking,* [38] Susan Cain says that "any time people come together in a meeting, we're not necessarily getting the best ideas; we're just getting the ideas of the best talkers . . . There's zero correlation between being the best talker and having the best ideas." [39]

Mashpee Wampanoag tribal leader and historian Joan Tavares Avant writes about the sacred power of the Talking Stick or Talking Feather used in Native American tribal courts and tribal circle meetings. These tools are used to instill listening and understanding. Only the person holding the Talking Stick or Feather speaks, and everyone else listens respectfully until the speaker is finished.

"Passing a Talking Stick with everyone stating their name and the reason why they have come sets the circle for a well-intentioned meeting, even if it is for decision-making, brainstorming, or conflict resolution," writes Tavares Avant. "As a result, at meetings or ceremonies, no one is left out of the process unless they have no comment." [40]

She also points out the dangers of multiple people speaking at once in a meeting. "Oftentimes decisions are made based on what we think we heard because more than one person may be speaking, which can lead to a damaged decision."

The concept of passing an object to speak and keep order in a group also appears in literature. If you or your kids were ever assigned to read William Golding's 1954 classic *Lord of the Flies*, about a group of British schoolboys marooned on an island and their gradual deterioration from social order into savagery, you may remember the significance in the novel of the conch shell. After finding the shell on the beach, the boys use it in

---

38 Learn more at https://www.quietrev.com/quiet-the-book-2/

39 https://www.ted.com/talks/susan_cain_the_power_of_introverts?language=en

40 https://indiancountrytoday.com/uncategorized/
talking-stick-and-feather-indigenous-tools-hold-sacred-power-of-free-speech

their meetings. Whoever holds the conch shell has the right to speak. This symbol becomes "an actual vessel of political legitimacy and democratic power," until the boys inadvertently destroy it, "signifying the demise of the civilized instinct" among the group.[41]

A few Policy Circles tried using the indigenous method of passing a Talking Stick (well, Talking Ring) at their circle meetings to great success! They found that passing around and holding something physical makes the person speaking aware that she is "holding court." The talking ring evolved into a two-minute hourglass that is now a key part of the Policy Circle's roundtable discussion model. The hourglass is a visual indicator of the time used speaking. Practicing to express your thoughts in fewer than two minutes is a great skill to develop.

The other piece of the process that is helpful to Policy Circles is the discussion guide, constructed in three rounds:

Round 1 is when circle participants each tell about themselves and present their "lens of care," or where they are coming from on this issue. It may be your business, your community experience, or your family. In a recent policy-circle discussion on government regulations, a person shared how regulations killed her ability to run her business. Another shared about new neighborhood regulations on the height of mailboxes and how a neighbor goes around to report those who do not meet the regulation. Yet another participant talked about regulations that are not respected around water usage and sanitation.

Round 2 is a more open discussion on major issues related to the topic in the community. In the case of the discussion on government regulations, the circle members discussed the impact of regulations on the community, government, and local businesses. They considered questions like "Is there an appropriate level of regulation?" This part of the discussion looks at broader community impact—how any given issue impacts others, rather than just one person.

Round 3 is about taking action and digging deeper into one issue. Actions could be as simple as talking to neighbors and others in your community or learning more about the impact, or they could be more involved, like speaking up publicly at a local government meeting or on the opinion page

---

41 See https://www.sparknotes.com/lit/flies/themes/

of your local paper. In the case of the discussion of regulations, participants were encouraged to investigate community programs, research their elected representatives' positions on those regulations, establish a relationship with those elected officials by communicating with them, or submit an op-ed or letter to the editor to their local paper. In other words, learning more and then putting what they have learned into action.

From there, some participants might take things even further. The Policy Circle website offers resources for developing a message about any given issue and guidance on steps like organizing a petition to amplify your voice and raise awareness.

From her involvement with a coalition of business owners, Policy Circle Leader Nicole Cline was asked to facilitate a community forum with the Missouri Department of Transportation (MODOT) on a traffic change measure. Nicole used the Policy Circle method of giving each community member three minutes to speak and for MODOT three minutes to respond. The result was a highly productive one-hour exchange between an agency and the community.

Yes, trusting the process will take a while, but in that process, you grow. Sometimes, you may not even know what you think about a particular issue until you go through this process of learning, discussing, and ultimately acting upon what you've discovered. But doing something like calling your representatives or writing an op-ed will help you to strengthen and trust your voice, ultimately bringing positive change in the world. Saying yes and stepping into new experiences benefits you and the world around you. And that is what we'll dive into in the next chapter.

Trust Challenge:

Have you ever used a decision matrix? What is one decision you have to make where this tool might be helpful?

Think about a group you're a part of that engages in group discussion—perhaps a book club, Bible study, a committee, or a Policy Circle. If you don't already, try using a two-minute hourglass or the Talking Stick (or some other object) at your next meeting. After trying it, discuss the following: What does this tool bring to your discussions? How does this tool help bring forth the ideas of quieter members?

Chapter 8

Trust Yourself as You Step Into New Experiences

Like many kids, I took piano lessons, briefly. When it became clear I didn't have a lot of interest in music, and possessed only an average amount of talent, I gave it up.

Fast-forward 40 years. My 50th birthday was approaching, and I heard a song on a podcast. It was a French love song, "*Dis quand reviendras tu?*" by Barbara. In English, "Say, when will you return?" interpreted by Hindi Zahra. It brought back memories of my childhood.

I loved the song, but I hadn't touched a piano for 40 years. I ordered the sheet music and decided that I would learn to play it. I was terrible. Sitting at my little electric keyboard, I felt hopeless. This was out of my comfort zone, and I was sure it would never sound like anything, let alone something I would play for a crowd at my birthday party.

But, I kept at it. I asked my children's piano instructor to work with me to help me learn it. I took the time to step away from the busyness of my life to study the music, to listen, to practice. I recorded myself and emailed it to a friend. I played it for my parents on FaceTime. One small step and then another carried me a little further each time.

I played the song at my birthday party. It wasn't perfect, but I had improved enough that I was willing to share it with my friends. And at The Policy Circle Summit, I played a recording of it during a talk I gave. I was able to improve through hard work and practice—and also by inviting others to share in the process.

That experience reminded me that to be good at something, you need to step out of your comfort zone. In other words, you need to make yourself uncomfortable—something most of us try to avoid. But learning to trust your voice means deliberately being uncomfortable. And, you need to connect with others in order to be better. And this is the heart of The Policy Circle.

The Policy Circle is about policy, but we discovered that it is really about strengthening high-level leadership abilities through policy conversations. And the first step to that is to trust yourself as you step into new experiences.

Rebuilding Trust

While I was writing this book, I would often watch the news with a sense of despair. The COVID pandemic, racial tensions, economic fallout—it all was overwhelming. What could I do, especially in these unprecedented times?

I wanted to have a conversation on the racial tensions, even though I knew it might be uncomfortable. As co-founder of The Policy Circle, I assembled four African-American and four Caucasian women from DC, Nashville, Chicagoland, Dallas, and Topeka, Kansas, to participate in a 90-minute virtual Policy Circle. My goal was to facilitate a conversation to unpack the racial tensions and unrest in our society, but also to engage in a conversation that sheds a light at the end of the tunnel. "Where Do We Go From Here: (Re)building Trust in America" was the theme of our Policy Circle conversation.

Prior to the meeting, everyone adhered to The Policy Circle framework and reviewed The Policy Circle brief "Credibility in Crisis: Rebuilding Trust in America." The brief cited facts and data to ground our conversation around trust in citizens, institutions, the media, education system, and businesses.

Everyone felt slightly nervous about this conversation, which definitely expanded the comfort zone of accomplished women. The Policy Circle framework kicked off the discussion, allowing everyone to introduce themselves and share the unique perspective and experience they each brought to the conversation. This introduction allowed us to share where we were coming from professionally *and* personally. Acknowledging a person and their unique history is the first step to building relationships.

Then, going around the Zoom panel, we each shared our views on the state of trust in our communities and our nation. Next, we each shared one or two priorities to be addressed to move forward and personal actions that we would take to heal tensions and change the narrative.

Here are some facts and statistics around trust, which we laid out as part of our conversation:

- Law Enforcement: Americans' levels of trust in law enforcement differ by demographics. Thirty percent of Blacks have confidence in the police, versus 61 percent of whites and 45 percent of Hispanics.
- Business: According to a Morning Consult poll, 55 percent of Americans say they trust the average American company, but 60 percent of U.S. adults say corruption is widespread in business. The 2019 Gallup Confidence in Institutions survey found small businesses, in particular, have Americans' trust, with 68 percent of U.S. adults saying they have "a great deal" of trust in small businesses.
- Government: According to the January 2020 Edelman Trust Barometer, 54 percent of Americans say they trust their state and local governments to do what is right, while only 43 percent of Americans have the same trust in the federal government. America is not alone. A 2017 global survey by Pew Research of 38 countries found a median of only 14 percent of the global population say they trust their national government a lot.
- Media: According to the Knight Foundation, the proportion of Americans with a great deal or fair amount of trust in the media fell from 54 to 32 percent between 2003 and 2016, and 69 percent of U.S. adults reported their trust in the news media has

decreased in the past decade. A full 75 percent of respondents cited bias, and 66 percent cited inaccuracy as reasons for this decrease. And 57 percent feel that social media divides us instead of uniting us.

- Community: In the U.S., levels of trust are not as high as global averages, with approximately 35 percent of Americans believing "most people can be trusted" and 64 percent saying people "need to be very careful" around others, according to the World Values Survey.

We agreed that trust was at the root of the current tensions and that based on personal experiences of being treated differently, some of us felt that trust has never been strong for all Americans toward all Americans. At the heart of the solution is building trust—not only in our institutions but in each other.

For trust to be established, all parties must feel that they are equal. Personal experiences of bias make it difficult to feel equal and have trust in law enforcement, government, business, and people. Quentella shared her son's question: "Why are stories at school about Blacks always sad?" That comment led us to discuss how joyful stories and accomplishments of Black entrepreneurs, scientists, bankers, and innovators, today and throughout history, need to be recognized, celebrated, and promoted so they become part of our nations' culture and public narrative.

There is no other country that offers so many opportunities to its citizens. America is not perfect, but we must all work diligently toward its ideal. The media constantly reinforces stories of injustices and racism instead of stories of opportunities, success, and warm relationships. Discussing and acknowledging injustices and historical racism is a good start to pave the way for change, but positive actions have to be taken to eliminate biases and racism and create a trustworthy society. Those positive actions and stories have to be elevated.

Our conversation fostered trust. Everyone shared their logic and was authentic. The third round of our discussion focused on actions to build a trustworthy society. Here are some of the actions that our participants are engaged in personally, with their family and in their communities and businesses:

- Change attitudes and narratives in schools and the media by supporting and promoting Black scholars and leaders who came together under a collective called 1776unites.com to tell the stories of a Black culture that embraces education, entrepreneurship, family, and happiness in seizing opportunities that enrich lives.
- Stop finger-pointing and diversify the people that you are with to enrich your perspectives. Lead constructive conversations and invite people who don't look like you to engage in meaningful conversations that build lasting relationships. It may be a book club, a prayer service, an educational session, or a Policy Circle. One woman of color, Karen Wells, is the CEO of Bridge Communities. She started a "Let's talk about it" group with her mostly white colleagues.
- Bring to the table people whose voices are not heard so they can be heard and feel part of the solution and the community.
- Take the time to understand others and have empathy for their experiences to ignite their potential. For example, Project One Ten in Chicago helps Black and brown boys successfully transition from middle school to high school through academic coaching and mentorship.
- Be honest with ourselves and see our own biases that we may not know we have. One participant is planning to launch a podcast "Creating Conversations," modeling conversations with diverse points of view.
- Get out of our media bubble and seek other points of view. Media is a huge part of the divide in our country. Let's swim counter-current and change the cancel culture of the media.

Trust is built on relationships. Relationships grow out of meaningful conversations where people have a chance to speak and to listen. At home, at work, within our networks, let's create those spaces to invite those conversations where all voices can be heard and ideas can be shared with real people in real time. At the risk of sounding overly optimistic, you can be the change that you want to see.

The women in that virtual Policy Circle took a chance and said yes to what they knew might be an uncomfortable conversation. But we came away from it better informed, not just about the facts but about the experiences of others. We grew not only in understanding but in empathy. When we trust, we can feel empathy, and we can begin to advocate for change.

In his book Atomic Habits, Jim Clear illustrates how small changes can have a big impact. He explains that if a pilot during takeoff decided to adjust course 3.5 degrees to the south, the plane's nose would move just a few feet. No one on board would notice the small change in direction. But over the course of a journey across the country, a plane set to go from Los Angeles to New York would instead land in Washington D.C. Positive change requires patience, consistency, and confidence that a new habit is keeping you on the right trajectory.[42]

Always Learning

In 2013, I was working out with a personal trainer, Meg Buckland. She was such an interesting person, and I learned a lot from her, far beyond just the coaching she gave during our workouts.

Meg's clients included the Center for Enriched Living in Riverwoods, Illinois, where she provided fitness training for people with intellectual disabilities. She told me how even incremental improvements in physical fitness helped people with intellectual disabilities to function better in every area of life. Some people have trouble bending over to tie their shoes. Their poor physical fitness had nothing to do with their intellectual disability. It was just the lack of daily movement that impacted their physical fitness and resulted in low stamina, obesity, joint issues, and general irritability.

We decided we would build an app that would allow primarily people with intellectual disabilities to engage in movement through role-play.

In deciding to say yes to this challenge, I took a risk. When we step out into new experiences, we are not guaranteed success. But by stepping out, I learned things that served me well down the road. And so, Foov Fitness was born (www.foovfitness.com). The name combines the words Fun and Move.

---

42 Cleary, James. *Atomic Habits: An Easy and Proven Way to Build Good Habits and Break Bad Ones.* New York: Avery/Penguin House. 2018.

Our app was simple. It simulated going to a ball game, and role playing a fan going to the game, an umpire, or a player. We wrote a whole script that became a workout, simulating going to a game: finding your seat, running the bases, hitting a home run, sweeping off home plate before the batter steps up.

It worked—it was engaging. People with intellectual disabilities ran the bases, sprinted, cheered. My heart still melts when I remember one non-verbal person laughing and running the bases back and forth with Meg 35 times! Or another person, who started singing "Take Me Out To The Ball Game," and then pretended to take a break and eat peanuts.

Kids like to pretend, but adults develop an inhibition about pretending or acting. However, we noticed that those inhibitions were nonexistent with adults with intellectual disabilities. They knew they were pretending but enjoyed it, and it motivated them to run and move. It was a way to build a connection around a common experience. We received some great comments from users.

However, we also faced some unexpected hurdles to overcome. One of the biggest challenges we faced was getting trainers, family members, or caregivers to use the app, to guide the person with intellectual disabilities through the activities on the app. Engaging in a workout built around pretending was hard for caregivers. Plus, the non-disabled adults found it repetitive. They wanted it to be more competitive, with scores, games, engagement. But for people with intellectual disabilities, the simplicity of it was appealing. It was a script they could follow as well as improvise on.

Beyond the hesitations of our buyer to embrace pretend play, we were a little out of our depth. Although Meg worked with clients with intellectual disabilities, we didn't have a strong network of people in that space. I was a complete newcomer. I hadn't studied fitness, I just enjoyed being physically fit. I didn't have a child or family member with intellectual disabilities. I just wanted to help. My partner had a little bit of a network but didn't have business experience. I had business experience but not the academic credentials required at the time to have an endorsed product. Foov Fitness didn't take off in the way we had hoped, and the next step would have been to sponsor an academic study to prove the concept.

Can you relate? Have you ever jumped into a project where your enthusiasm outweighed your expertise? On our way to discovering our voice, we may have to sing off-key once in a while.

But, it was still an incredibly valuable experience. Because when I went to start The Policy Circle, I knew what *not* to do. I learned so much by trying things that didn't quite work as I expected. That, too, is part of learning how to trust your voice. You have to trust that even if your grand plan does not succeed, just engaging in the process moves you forward. You must commit to learning, whether by success or by your mistakes. Every experience can be a learning experience if you are willing to say yes and trust the process.

Initiating the Foov project brought my attention to people that we often forget—adults with intellectual disabilities and their families. How do we create career pathways for them so they can lead productive lives, be members of our communities? How do we lighten the administrative burden of small and large businesses so they can employ people with intellectual disabilities? In testing the app, we interacted with people with intellectual disabilities, we asked them for feedback, and we gave them a voice.

Here's what I learned:

- Surround yourself with the right partners: know-how, network, operations, and financial sustainability.
- Know who your buyer is and what problem are you solving for them (with Foov, our user was not our buyer. And that buyer did not see fitness as a problem nor a priority).
- Listen to your users and buyers and be agile. You are not the user.
- Secure investors in the project.

So, the next time you try something and it doesn't work out quite the way you want, or even if it seems to fail, consider the fact that the experience was still one of incomparable value. If you can step back and see your mistakes, you can also assess what you did right. If you are willing to look at it calmly, you can apply what you learned to future endeavors.

Here's another important lesson I learned: When you start a new project, you need to bring people to the table that have different skill sets. You need a strong network in the space where you hope to make an impact—something we lacked when we started Foov Fitness.

But The Policy Circle was different. I had learned that trusting your own voice does not mean you have to do everything all by yourself. Trusting your own voice means knowing your strengths and also inviting others to bring their strengths to the table, working together to build something that none of you could do by yourself.

My friend and neighbor Beth Feeley was really the instigator of The Policy Circle. She is the one who suggested we bring together a group of women after that first conference we attended. After the first few meetings and the growing interest, we realized that we were on to something bigger, that people wanted to be heard. Beth joined the team and developed Policy Circle briefs with expert policy editors. Through publishing and leading discussions on The Policy Circle brief on poverty, Beth met Bob Woodson, a civil rights activist and champion of entrepreneurial values for the Black community. His network of community-based organizations around the country transformed lives and gave people a second chance.

Beth noticed that the neighborhood high school, in their attempt to appease the guilt of the prosperous, portrayed African Americans only as victims, not as thought leaders, entrepreneurs, and scientists. She set out to change the narrative and became Bob Woodson's implementer.

Beth was instrumental in assembling a coalition of Black scholars and leaders, who formed 1776unites.org and published a curriculum to tell the success story of Blacks in America, the stories of joy that kids want to identify with, that bring hope and shine the light on role models.

Beth also formed a neighborhood committee that reports and activates citizens on the policies set by the school boards, township and the village. Beth deserves a medal of recognition for her passion, her focus, and her relentless tenacity to hold representatives accountable to excellence for the community.

I could not have kept going without Beth's help. And then, I met Angela Braly and Kathy Hubbard, and again, teamwork helped us to move forward. Angela had a large corporate perspective—her focus was on building a scalable and repeatable framework. Kathy had a great network. And I'm an implementer. We each brought something to the table, we all expanded our comfort zone.

Trust Challenge:

 How are you expanding your comfort zone? Think of a project or venture you engaged in that didn't succeed in the way you'd hoped (like the experience with the FoovFitness app). What key lessons did you learn? How were you able to apply what you learned in later situations?

In this chapter, we read: "Trust is built on relationships. Relationships grow out of meaningful conversations where people have a chance to speak and to listen." Who do you need to invite into meaningful conversation so that you can build trust?

PART TWO

EXPANDING YOUR INFLUENCE

As you build trust in yourself and others, you have the opportunity to expand your influence by engaging in enriching discussions.

The Policy Circle is an invitation to discuss public policy. These discussions don't just inform us about important issues. They teach participants how to engage in discussions about anything, in any context. This builds both competence and confidence. How will you use your voice to influence others in your community and in the world?

In Part One, we built a foundation, and now, we're going to get very practical and talk about how to make a difference through dialogue.

Chapter 9

Trust That You Can Facilitate Dialogue

The Policy Circle provides an environment to develop facilitation skills that can be taken to a broader audience and applied to more complex issues. A constructive conversation, which ultimately yields influence, begins with asking questions to seek understanding of all perspectives and drive to an approach where everyone feels heard and included. Here's how to facilitate constructive dialogue on any topic:

- Determine the type of interaction you want to engage in.
- Acknowledge your desire to understand various perspectives.
- Assess your values.
- Recognize the lenses through which you view the world and the issue at hand.
- Cultivate empathy by considering the other person's point of view.

Let's unpack each of these.

Determine the type of interaction you want to engage in. The way we speak and listen impacts our interaction. If we approach a conversation as a debate, our goal often becomes winning that debate. We're focused on convincing the other person that we are right. We listen only enough to refute what they say. Ironically, when we debate, we might think we've "won" when we have actually shut down real communication. Difficult conversations become even more difficult when we frame them as a debate.

If we have a discussion, that's a step in the right direction. Merriam-Webster defines discussion as "consideration of a question in open and usually informal debate." When we come to a difficult conversation with the goal of having meaningful dialogue, something shifts. Dialogue is defined as "an exchange of ideas and opinions; a discussion between representatives of parties to a conflict that is aimed at resolution."[43] Dialogue implies an exchange that is constructive in that it leads to something new. Discussion is simply "talking about it."

We seek to understand, to listen—not just to the words but to the emotions and concerns behind them. As we listen, we get curious about what is behind the other person's words. What fears are they wrestling with? What past events color the way they see the world and approach this conversation?

Dialogue invites us away from accusations and assumptions. We use "I feel…" instead of "you should…" or "you always…." We don't assign motives or blame the other person but strive for empathy. We let go of having to win, and in so doing, we actually make more progress toward consensus and a common goal.

Acknowledge your desire to understand various perspectives. What if, even though you think a certain issue is cut-and-dried, you have not considered all sides of it? Even when you think that there is only one "right" answer about that issue, other people might see it differently.

To set the right tone, you have to let go of "Right, Righteous, Certain" and acknowledge that you possibly do not have the perspective of every part of a complex issue. This is not about saying you're right or wrong, but you're simply moving into a space where you genuinely want to understand other perspectives. Why does another person hold the view that they do? When you let go of being certain about something and seek to understand someone else, conversations become more constructive.

Assess your values. If you're not sure how to define your values, think about what you worry about. As Jonathan Haidt outlines: care, liberty,

43 See https://www.merriam-webster.com/dictionary/

loyalty, fairness, authority, sanctity. What do you worry the most about: liberty/choice/responsibility, economics/sustainability, immediate relief of suffering, or rules and safety? What do you worry about in each of these areas?

Recognize your "lenses" and sphere of care. As we discussed earlier, we all view the world through different lenses. What lenses are you wearing, and what is your sphere of care: me, immediate relationships, organizations, community, nation, humanity, future generations, all life? Here's an example. During the 2020 pandemic, some local governments prohibited landlords from evicting tenants who could not pay their rent. If you are a renter, you see the world through that lens. You think, I have lost my job, I'm quarantined, the economy is shut down. I have no way of making money, and I can't pay my rent.

But if you are a landlord, you see the issue through a different lens. Perhaps the property you own has a mortgage, and you will fall behind on paying the mortgage if you don't receive rent payments. If the bank forecloses, both you and the renter will be out of luck. Perhaps you think that the government should prevent banks from foreclosing.

Perhaps another person outside of the situation might be concerned about how many people will become homeless if they are all evicted and the impact that would have on society. Different lenses mean different perspectives, and if we are aware of our lens and our sphere of care, we will move forward into meaningful dialogue.

Understanding other people's lenses helps you to cultivate empathy. What approach, values, and lens is the person looking through when they engage in conversation with you? Equally important to ensuring that you are approaching a conversation from an aware and constructive manner is understanding and relating to the perspective of the person you are speaking with.

Cultivate empathy by considering the other person's point of view. When discussing issues, make it your goal to be a conversation partner, not an interrogator or a pushy salesperson for your own point of view. Try to use phrases like "I appreciate what you are saying" or "I hadn't thought of it that way, that is interesting." Or "I'm curious about . . . Can you tell me more about that?"

In their book *How to Have Impossible Conversations*, authors Peter Boghossian and James Lindsay explain that conversations break down when someone wants to be the "messenger of truth." Don't make this mistake. It will actually shut down meaningful dialogue. Instead, focus on being a learner. Your goal for the conversation is not to convince but to learn and to assume the person you're talking to can teach you something. Assume the best intentions in your conversation partner, Boghossian and Lindsay advise.[44]

I have found that shifting your thinking to focus on listening, learning, and dialogue really does change conversation. When you model this behavior, the other person is more likely to do the same. That will result in you not having to be defensive or get frustrated, and as a result, you'll feel more sure of yourself, even in situations where you're a little uncertain. In other words, showing respect and listening carefully to others will help you to trust your own voice more fully.

Instilling Doubt

Even after taking these steps to improve dialogue, some conversations can still be difficult. Over the years, I've invited hundreds of women into discussions of policy. I've found that it's easy to discuss almost any issue with people who agree with you! The hard part is when you must tackle a conversation with those who see things very differently. It can feel impossible.

In their book, authors Boghossian and Lindsay offer practical guidance, beginning with this: Don't try to change anyone's mind. It will only frustrate you (and the other person). Instead, simply make it your goal to instill doubt. Get the other person to simply question their hard held beliefs, and you'll take an important step of opening dialogue.

But how do you even begin to instill doubt? They suggest beginning not with statements (of your opinions or the facts as you see them) but with questions instead. Try to find out exactly what the other person thinks. While you engage them, follow these guidelines:

- Model the behavior you want to see in others. Don't be rude or pushy. Listen if you want to be listened to.

---

44 Peter Boghossian and James Lindsay. *How to Have Impossible Conversations*. New York: Hachette Book Group. 2019.

- Define words that are discussed. Avoid jargon.
- Ask for explanations, but do so without demands or threats.
- Shift from blame to contribution—"What factors contributed to [X]?"
- Use questions like these to ask where their knowledge comes from:
    –"That's an interesting perspective. What leads you to conclude that?"
    –"Would every reasonable person draw the same conclusion? I'm a reasonable person, and I'm having trouble drawing the same conclusions. –How do I get there?"
    –"Can you please give me an example of some other issue where you use that same reasoning process?"

Sometimes the way you phrase things can either deepen the conversation or shut it down. Here are some practical phrases to use when trying to engage in difficult conversations:

- "I hear you. I wonder if we can get around our disagreement by looking at it another way."
- "I know that my... may be perceived as... but how do we solve...?"
- "These issues are really frustrating, I know. They get to me too."
- Speak about ideas and beliefs, not people—"that or one's" instead of "you."
- "I'm skeptical" instead of "I disagree."
- "Ultimately we are both interested in... but don't see eye-to-eye on how to achieve those goals. Can we talk more directly about the ways we can achieve a balance?"
- "That's right" instead of "Yes" signals understanding of a position. Always say "Yes, and..." instead of "Yes, but..."
- Figure out how confident someone is in a belief by asking, "On a scale of one to ten, how confident are you that X is true?" Or ask, "How important is this issue versus this other issue?" Or share your thoughts in a way that invites dialogue, by saying something like, "I'm a three on the scale that X is true. I'm not

sure how I'd get to where you are at a nine. I want to see what I'm missing."

- Ask "How do you know that?" so that the person can cite their sources, essentially telling you whose expert opinion you can read to gather more information.

Discussing policy (or any other topic people care deeply about) can be difficult but not impossible. A conversation is productive when we find common objectives to move the needle on the issue at hand and identify concrete actions that we agree on. To have a constructive conversation, we need to have a road map that answers the following questions:

1. **Where are we going?** Let's agree on the destination and route, i.e., the goal and data we're using.

2. **Who is going with us?** Who are the stakeholders impacted here and which one are we focused on in our conversation? If you are leading discussion at the community level, it would be a good idea to list all the stakeholders and ensure that they are represented throughout the effort. What is the role of individual community members?

3. **How are we getting there?** What's the role of technology and infrastructure? Do we have a timeline? Is there a new or existing technology that will have an impact in the short and long run? What can be done to speed up development or adoption?

4. **How much does it cost?** What are the costs of development, implementation, and maintenance of the initiatives associated with a policy? How will those costs be managed and covered?

5. **How do we know we've arrived?** How do we know when we are successful and when we are not? What metrics do we need to pay attention to, and what do those measurements tell us? What happens if the policy is unsuccessful? Is there a plan to sunset a program?

"Not in My Backyard"

How does this work in practical terms? Let's look at a real-life situation where local officials missed an opportunity because they did not engage in constructive conversations. This is an example of what happens when we don't engage all the stakeholders on a decision that will impact them.

The village of Itasca is a suburb of Chicago, home to just 8,700 people. The village board was considering a request from a substance abuse and mental health provider, Haymarket, to convert a vacant hotel in Itasca into a behavioral health clinic, which would offer substance abuse and mental health treatment for adults 18 and over. Haymarket, which operated other facilities in the Chicago area, planned to spend $1.5 million to retrofit the hotel.

According to public health experts, addiction and other mental health issues were becoming a large (though perhaps well hidden) problem in the suburbs. People often had to travel out of state to receive treatment. The area did not have another option for those needing mental health treatment, and Haymarket planned to respond to the high demand for the services the facility would provide. There were no other plans on the table to reopen the hotel or convert it to another use.

While there is unquestionably a need for mental health treatment facilities, especially in the suburbs, and the project would have created jobs for the village, it ultimately was voted down, despite being endorsed by more than 60 elected officials, government agencies, healthcare providers, community organizations, and individuals. Why did that happen? In part, the developers failed to engage in meaningful dialogue (not just providing information, but also listening) with all the stakeholders, particularly the residents of the town of Itasca.

Itasca residents essentially said, "Not in my backyard" to the project, in large part because they were not invited into the conversation at the beginning. They objected to having the facility close to parks and schools where children would gather. They voiced concerns about the impact on local emergency services. They were frightened by what they thought a "mental health and drug rehab facility" would look like and what sort of people it would bring to their town.

A letter from the mayor of Itasca also complained of Haymarket's "lack of transparency" and said its plans for the property were "cloaked in secrecy." With that letter, he sent a list of questions about funding, security, staffing, community outreach, and more. While Haymarket maintains that they responded to all of the questions, it apparently was too late. People had already made up their minds about the project.

In my discussion with then DuPage County board member Greg Hart, who served at the time as co-chairman of DuPage's Heroin/Opioid Prevention and Education Taskforce, and Kim Walz, who is on the board of Haymarket, the project was meeting a community need based on the data. However, the residents did not see the roles that they could have played. They could have been teachers, mentors, or volunteers and lead awareness campaigns about mental health and addiction. Instead, they only imagined drug addicts wandering in their neighborhoods, parks, and schools. Conversations with local influencers and key stakeholders did not happen, so they rejected the project.

A Framework for Developing Policy

Policymaking happens in two phases, in my opinion. The first phase is a consultation phase where people share their concerns, their views, their priorities. In a sense, The Policy Circle model lends itself to prepare people to participate in the policymaking process.

At every Policy Circle meeting, we use the same framework. Our members have come to rely upon and trust this framework, which provides structure and safety in our discussions. People know they won't be attacked or shut down. Rather, they will listen to others and trust that others will listen to them.

The second phase of policy making is developing the actual policy that will impact private and business behavior. Here's the framework that allows the development of sound policy. This framework could be used as the agenda of a task force.

Goal and Vision. We begin with questions that guide us toward our goals and vision. We ask:

- What are the measurable and realistic goals?
- Who are the stakeholders?
- What "lens of care" is each stakeholder wearing?
- What are the vision and goals of the initiative/issue?
- What data are we relying on?
- How do we evaluate data?

- Are there good success models to build on?
- Are all voices directly present?
- What is already being done about this?

Role of Communities. Then we look at roles and community members who have a stake in the outcomes of whatever policy we are discussing. We examine the following questions:

- What values and principles are at play? (choice, innovation, immediate relief, growth, etc.)
- What existing laws and regulations need to be taken into consideration?
- What are the opportunities for individual community members to be directly involved?
- Are there contradictions?

Innovation and Infrastructure. From there, we explore the innovation and infrastructure that might have an impact on the policy. We ask:

- What is the role of current technology in this issue?
- What is the impact and direction of future technology?
- Is there an existing infrastructure or should a new one be developed?
- Are we embracing technology?

Measures of Success. Ultimately, we want to measure the impact of a given policy, as well as the impact of changing that policy. Here, we examine the following:

- How do we define and measure success?
- How do we measure failure?
- What are the unintended consequences based on human behavior?
- How will the initiative be remediated or sunsetted?

Cost and Benefits. Once we know these impacts, we can accurately discuss the cost/benefits.

- What is the cost of development?
- What is the cost of implementation?
- What is the cost of ongoing support?
- Who will pay? Is it viable long term?
- Are there societal costs?

Once we know the costs and benefits, it's important to understand who the stakeholders are and who is paying the cost and getting the benefit. Some people who might possibly be impacted by the policy include:

- Families
- Senior citizens
- People with different abilities
- Lower, middle, or high-income individuals (Is each impacted differently or similarly? In what ways?)
- Large and small businesses
- Civic institutions such as local, state, and federal governments
- E-commerce businesses

Conclusion

In these chapters, I went through the gusts of wind that make the flywheel turn to help you build confidence in yourself to trust your voice and your trajectory. I hope that you use this book as a reference to practice strengthening the trust you have in yourself.

Strength, power, and confidence are built daily. So, go back to a chapter each month and view it as a workout to focus on. Use the "Trust Challenge" at the end of each chapter to strengthen trust.

Here's a review of the topics we covered in Part One:

Trust: How can we build it?
Trust the features of human nature, your values, strengths, and blind spots
Trust that you are building something bigger than you
Trust that your voice will spark others
Trust your mind and spirit
Trust that you can build a strong network
Trust in the process, even if it takes a while
Saying yes and stepping out into new experiences

The second part of the book is a tool to engage constructively. Copy the agenda for the next task force that you join, and use it as a roadmap. Read and reread and practice having impossible conversations with everyone that you encounter. You will find that giving someone a voice, a space to be heard, is one of the most memorable and precious gifts that you can give.

During the five years that it took to build The Policy Circle from an idea to a real organization with a team and an executive director, I grew more than I did in 25 years of professional life. My network expanded and continues to grow here in the U.S. and abroad. The Policy Circle framework is being used, for example, by the International Republican Institute (IRI) in its Arab Women's Leadership Institute, a network to engage and advance the rights of Arab women and promote participation in the political process.

The Policy Circle started casually in my living room with only the ambition to bring women together to be informed. We focused on women because even though we are 51 percent of the population, women were in 2021 only 20-25 percent of all elected officials in all levels of government, and less than 10 percent of CEOs of Fortune 500 in the U.S.

We called it The Policy Circle so that it will continue to grow to be a framework and a platform for both men and women to start their journey of civic leadership.

THE FUNDAMENTALS

Instilling Doubt vs Changing Minds
ASK CLARIFYING QUESTIONS

- Model the behavior you want to see in others
- Define words that are discussed, avoid jargon
- Ask for explanations
- Shift from blame to contribution - "What factors contributed to [X]?"
- Ask where their knowledge comes from:
  - "That's an interesting perspective. What leads you to conclude that."
  - "Would every reasonable person draw the same conclusion?...."I'm a reasonable person and I'm having trouble drawing the same conclusions, how do I get there?"
  - "Can you please give me an example of some other issue where you use that same reasoning process?"

Mindset
BE A CONVERSATION PARTNER - "I APPRECIATE THAT"

- Have a goal for the conversation
- Assume best intentions in your conversation partner
- Start a conversation with wonder - "I want to learn..." Plan on investing in the relationship
- Listen more than you talk
- Don't be a messenger of truth

"NOBODY CARES HOW MUCH YOU KNOW UNTIL THEY KNOW HOW MUCH YOU CARE."

Improve your dialogue
DEEPEN THE CONVERSATION AND LET FRIENDS BE WRONG

- "I hear you ... I wonder if we can get around our disagreement by looking at it another way."
- "I know that my ... may be perceived as ... but how do we solve ..."
- "These issues are really frustrating, I know. They get to me too."
- Speak about ideas and beliefs, not people: "that or one's" instead of "you"
- "I'm skeptical" instead of "I disagree"
- "Ultimately we are both interested in .... But don't see eye-to-eye on how to achieve those goals. Can we talk more directly about the ways we can achieve a balance?"
- "That's right" instead of "Yes" signals understanding of a position - always say "Yes AND" instead of "Yes BUT"
- Figure out how confident someone is in a belief:
  - On a scale of "1-10" how confident are you that X is true? Or how important is this issue vs another issue? Ask "I'm a 3 on a 1 to 10 scale that X is true. I'm not sure how I'd get to where you are at a 9. I want to see what I'm missing."
- 'How do you know that?" - whose expert opinion can I read to gather more information. Who are the 3 best experts who disagree/agree with that position?
- Rapoport's rule - before rebuttal you must:
  - Restate their position better than they said it and list points of agreement.

"Why would or wouldn't someone be a bad person if they didn't hold that belief?"

SOURCE: JAMES LINDSEY & PETER BOGHOSSIAN AUTHORS OF HOW TO HAVE IMPOSSIBLE CONVERSATIONS FUNDAMENTALS SHEET WAS PREPARED BY THEPOLICYCIRCLE.ORG

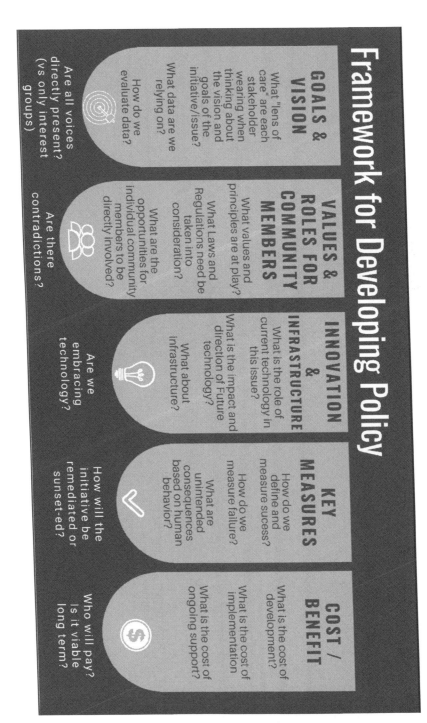

Framework for Developing Policy

GOALS & VISION

What "lens of care" are each stakeholder wearing when thinking about the vision and goals of the initiative/issue?

What data are we relying on?

How do we evaluate data?

VALUES & ROLES FOR COMMUNITY MEMBERS

What values and principles are at play?

What Laws and Regulations need be taken into consideration?

What are the opportunities for individual community members to be directly involved?

INNOVATION & INFRASTRUCTURE

What is the role of current technology in this issue?

What is the impact and direction of Future technology?

What about infrastructure?

KEY MEASURES

How do we define and measure success?

How do we measure failure?

What are unintended consequences based on human behavior?

COST / BENEFIT

What is the cost of development?

What is the cost of implementation

What is the cost of ongoing support?

Who will pay? Is it viable long term?

Are all voices directly present? (vs only interest groups)

Are there contradictions?

Are we embracing technology?

How will the initiative be remediated or sunset-ed?

Acknowledgments

- Keri Wyatt Kent, without whom this project would not have become a reality. You believed in the theme and in my voice, and you did not give up on me.
- My co-founders of The Policy Circle, Angela Braly and Kathy Hubbard, with whom I created a framework to engage more women in policy-making dialogue because we believe that the free-enterprise system creates opportunities for everyone, especially the most vulnerable. Laura Cox Kaplan who so generously shares her network and model excellence in all her endeavours.
- All The Policy Circle members and supporters who inspired me by believing in the model and the value that The Policy Circle delivers.
- The first Policy Circle members from whom I learned so much: Beth Feeley who said, "Why don't we just bring women in the neighborhood together?" and those who all shared insights, supported the program, showed up, stepped up, and led—Stacey Woerhle, Lisa Carter, Darcy Powers, Joan Lasonde, Jasmine Hauser, Tracy Bosman, Molly Ervin, Coco Harris, and Danielle Merger, Louise Sandborn, Anne Williams.
- The Policy Circle team: Kristin Jackson, who helps me navigate policy making and brought on board Corrine Winters,

the amazingly diligent policy editor. Molly Ervin, who built the infrastructure and contributed her process expertise. Nicole Cline, who trusted the model, trusted me, and worked tirelessly to expand the organization. Kim Borchers, who spearheaded the creation of the Civic Leadership Engagement Roadmap. Judi Willard who brings warmth, humor, and confidence to all circle leaders. Janet Burt and Stacy Blakeley, who are taking the Policy Circle to the next level nationally and globally.

- Lorna McMahon, who is like my pacer in a bike race who keeps up and refills water bottles, fixes flats, and never loses her cool. She makes everything happen.
- Brian Baker and Lauren Kirshner, who push me to expand my comfort zone in every way, and every day.
- Of course, my parents. When I shared with my dad the framework on policy making, he said, "This is really good. You need to share this; it is a contribution to society." He is also the one who made me realize that The Policy Circle was actually the execution of his vision of "kitchen cells" to enable public consultation. My mom is my biggest fan and an amazing role model. She never stops learning, trying new things, and giving her all.
- My in-laws, the Ricketts family, who have embraced who I am and pushed my life to new planes.
- My kids, Félix, Pascale and Daphné, who have heard about The Policy Circle since its inception and have witnessed meetings, watched our videos, given feedback on the op-eds, and volunteered at events. I wrote this book for them, so it could be something to accompany them on their life journey.
- My husband, Todd, who asked, "Who drives your bus?" and who made me realize that I matter.

Made in the USA
Columbia, SC
29 August 2022

66290706R00074